THE MASTER CRAFT OF LIVING

by William L. Fischer

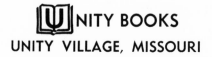

UNITY BOOKS

UNITY VILLAGE, MISSOURI

Contents

THE MASTER CRAFT OF
Relaxation

The idea of relaxation is something that is an involved part of the teachings of Jesus Christ. In the Sermon on the Mount, Jesus goes into quite a discourse about people who are concerned over what they shall eat and drink and how they shall be clothed. And then He says: "Which of you by being anxious can add a cubit to his span of life?" And one translation states it: "Which of you with taking thought . . ." What Jesus implies in this passage is that anxiety and stress simply add nothing constructive to a person's life. Any person who has ever tried to worry himself through a problem can testify that this is so.

If anxiety cannot accomplish anything constructive in our lives, then the antithesis of it should. That is, if a person can achieve the ability to approach life in a relaxed, confident, serene way, he stands a much better chance of living more satisfactorily. We are all trying to get a better grip on life. We might say, then, that there must be a letting go in order to gain a new hold. We must relax in order to be able to get a firmer grip on life.

There is a splendid illustration of this to be found in the functioning of the human heart. Do you realize that the human heart does 120 foot-tons of work every twenty-four hours? And, of course, it cannot suspend that activity for more than a few minutes of a person's entire lifetime, or that person will cease to live. In normal heart action diastole follows systole from seventy to seventy-five times a minute as long as you live. It is contraction, then relaxation; and the relaxation exceeds the contraction in the matter of actual time. It has been figured scientifically that the heart's relaxation time—the time it is resting between beats—amounts to fifteen hours out of the twenty-four-hour period. It is this rest schedule that enables the heart to go on working without stopping—sometimes for more than a hundred years.

Do you know what the heart is doing during that brief time of relaxation between beats? It is getting ready for the next effort. When you think about that, you can see the importance of developing the ability to relax. Anyone who wants to accomplish anything in life has to get ready for the next effort. Relaxation gives us that preparation. If you will look at the lives of most of the people who get things done in life, you will find that they are seldom the nervous, fussy, restless type. Rather, they are the kind of people who have a quietness, ease, and calmness about them. The whole secret of accomplishment in life lies with a relaxed approach to whatever task lies before us.

From our earliest childhood most of us have heard the expression, "Haste makes waste." It isn't that doing things quickly prohibits us from doing them well. Rather, it is that oftentimes when we do things quickly, we are doing them without making the necessary preparation of relaxation. And when we approach any task in a keyed-up, anxious state of mind, our chances of bungling it are much greater. Hence, we have found by experience that "haste makes waste."

One author said that hurry was the torture assigned to those souls who were on the outskirts of hell. His description was: "Hurry, hurry! Run, run! Rushing like the wind, always going somewhere but never getting anywhere, driven by stinging wasps and hornets!" Of course, this is descriptive writing. But let me assure you, any person who lives like that lives on the outskirts of hell. And not only that; he lives out of rhythm with all of nature.

Nature and creation have a tempo about them that includes the elements of relaxation and letting go. We can see this all about us: alternation, reciprocation, day and night, summer and winter, flow and ebb, flux and reflux, systole and diastole, action and reaction. This is the rhythm of life. If you break this rhythm by leaving relaxation out of your life, then you cannot possibly experience that state known as well-being. This is because well-being is a product of living in accord with the rhythm. The need for relaxation is valid, because it is built into the very nature of creation.

I remember one time when I was in my early teens and had learned to drive a car around the fields and meadows near my home. I wasn't old enough to drive on a public road, but I did drive off in the fields where no harm could be done. Some of the other boys of the same age did the same thing. Then one of the boy's sisters wanted us to teach her how to drive. So we showed her what the clutch was and how it operated, explained the gear shift, the emergency brake, and so forth, and turned her loose.

She did quite a remarkable job of it for a time, but then we noticed something rather alarming. Smoke began coming out from under the car. And we found that she had been driving around with the emergency brake on; or at least partly on. She had discovered that if she had that brake at least partly on, it enabled her to control the car a bit better. She had only to let her foot off the gas pedal, and the car was automatically slowed down. Of course, the result was that the brake lining burned off, and someone's dad was pretty angry.

I mention this because I think that this is the way a lot of people live. They live with a certain amount of tension all the time. And this is just like trying to drive a car with the brakes on. Something is bound to burn out. What happens is something like a short circuit in the emotional system of a person. When this occurs, the person who experiences it usually says, "My nerves are shot." After anyone has lived for a period of time under a pattern of stress, suffering the consequences of this, he comes to the place where his human tolerance for stress is lessened. From then on, it doesn't take nearly as much to unnerve that person. He simply cannot tolerate as much tension as he could previously.

Well, what can we do about it? If tension,

stress, and anxiety are detrimental to our well-being, how can they be dealt with successfully? There are a lot of temporary ways to do it. You can get your physician to prescribe some tranquilizers for you. But when they wear off, your problem will still be there.

Did you ever hear the story about the fellow who had a terrible headache every day? In the nighttime it went away. But every day it came back again, and he would have to take aspirin tablets all day long. But, as soon as the aspirin wore off, back came the headache. He tried to figure out what he did in the daytime that he didn't do at night that might cause this. One thing was that he wore a hat during the day. Then he discovered that his hat was too small! Now, if he had continued to wear a hat that was too small, he could have taken aspirin the rest of his life. He would still have had the headache, because he was dealing with the effect rather than the cause. By the same token, tranquilizers only quiet the *effect* of anxiety. They do not offer a permanent solution to the problem, because they do not remove the *cause* of the anxiety.

Another temporary way to handle anxiety is to take a vacation. But unfortunately, this does not usually deal with causes either. I remember one time when I was staying in a cottage along Lake Erie. In the next cottage was a man elaborately prepared for relaxation. He looked rather spent and like a man who needed to relax. One of the first things he did was string up a hammock. I could see that he was thinking that just to lull in that hammock represented the epitome of relaxation for him. He went inside and got himself a cold drink, came out, and crawled into his hammock.

In a little while I thought I would drop by, get somewhat acquainted with him, and have a friendly chat. Well, that man was lying in his hammock as if someone had starched him. He was so tense and rigid that I thought perhaps rigor mortis had set in. In a friendly way I said to him, "Hello, what are you doing?" And with his lips so tight they were white, he replied, "Relaxing." Obviously, he wasn't relaxing. Whatever had caused him to feel the need to get away, he must have brought it with him. That fellow was around for a week, and he never did bend very much in his hammock. So vacations do not really offer a permanent answer to tension, unless we learn to relax before we leave home.

Then there are persons who try to solve their relaxation needs by consuming alcohol. They feel that the depressant quality of alcohol will enable them to unwind a little bit. From a physiological point of view, they may be right. But this doesn't offer a permanent solution anymore than a tranquilizer does. After the narcotic effect of the alcohol wears off, the problem is still there. And added to the problem, there may well be a dandy hangover! So there is every reason to believe that, rather than solving any problems, alcohol only compounds them.

If these things indulged in by so many persons do not offer the permanent solution, what does? The only way any kind of a permanent solution can be evolved is if a change is made inside the person. After all, anxiety and tension are states of mind. And so they must be remedied in the mind. This is why real relaxation cannot be achieved if you start with the physical.

I think that the only permanent way to make adjustments in consciousness is through meditation and prayer. I think that there are definite steps that one must take in order to relax. And I want to give you those steps now, as a definite program or a devotional drill.

The first step is *meditation*. The dictionary says that meditation is contemplation. In this step, you must contemplate the things that are conducive to peace and serenity for yourself. And this, obviously, means that you must stop thinking about things that would detract from your peace of mind. You may want to recall some beautiful words of poetry, or the melody of a lovely old hymn. But it must be something to get your thinking away from topics of anxiety, and in accord with a consciousness of serenity. Incorporated in this step of meditation is the process of denial. You are denying a place in your mind to the negation of anxiety and tension. And this has a cleansing effect.

The next important step is *affirmation*. At this point you are ready to establish a definite, spiritual awareness of relaxation in your consciousness. My favorite affirmative prayer, which I call my spiritual tranquilizer, is: *"I am poised and centered in the Christ presence, and nothing can disturb the calm peace of my soul."*

Now you are sitting comfortably and your mind is properly conditioned. You speak this affirmation. You speak it several times. You speak it gently, but firmly. And you begin to feel something happening within you. You begin to feel a calmness come over you. With your mind relaxed, and a change taking place in your consciousness, this feeling begins to reflect itself through your body. From the crown of your head to the soles of your feet, everything lets go. And you feel a sense of personal serenity and relaxation that cannot be achieved in any other way.

Now you are ready for the final step in your program. It is the *silence*. The silence is a time of "feeling." You quietly feel the condition you have generated. During this time, you know the experience of perfect relaxation. The reason your relaxation is so complete is that it has been achieved through prayer. You have not just produced some human quality of peace. Rather, you have invited the very peace of God into your mind and body. You know that you have the spirit of peace within you. This spirit of peace is a part of your divine makeup. And through the steps that you have taken, you have brought this spirit of peace out of the potential and into the actual.

At this point, God is no longer an abstract being to you. God has become an actual experience. You will have achieved something that men have sought for ages to achieve. You will know the very feeling Jesus described, when He said: "Peace I leave with you; my peace I give to you; not as the world gives, do I give to you. Let not your hearts be troubled, neither let them be afraid." When you can do this, effectively, at any time you desire, you will have mastered the master craft of relaxation.

THE MASTER CRAFT OF
Forgiveness

One of the most misunderstood and seemingly difficult virtues of the spiritual life is the craft of forgiveness. Make no mistake about it, this is a master craft. Some people who think they are forgiving are very clumsy about it. What they consider to be forgiveness is far less than a master craft.

For instance, there are those who say, "I can forgive, but I can never forget." Others give token expression to forgiveness, but should a need to do so arise, they are quick to get an incident out of their mental file for reference. Still others may forgive someone who has wronged them, but if a second need

17

to forgive the same person arises, they refuse to repeat their forgiveness. These are just a few of the inadequate expressions of forgiveness. There are many, many more. ‐

The most common area of error is with this "forgive and forget" business. When the subject comes up, I think of a certain sales manager who was talking to a friend. He said, "Although I often get angry, I don't hold a grudge—not even against people who have done things to me that I'll *never* forget." Rather revealing, isn't it? If we cannot forget a thing, then we have not forgiven it either.

Some years ago my wife was teaching a Sunday-school class on the lesson-theme "Forgiving and Forgetting." She told the children that they should practice this idea throughout the week, and come back the following week to make a report about it. One little girl came up with a classic observation. She said, "But if we are supposed to forgive and forget, how can we remember to tell about it next week?"

Clara Barton, the founder of the American Red Cross, was once reminded about an especially cruel thing that had been done to her years before. But Miss Barton seemed not to recall the incident. "Don't you remember it?" her friend asked. "No," came the reply. "I distinctly remember forgetting that!"

When you think about it, one of the greatest agents working toward happiness in the world is forgiveness. Can you imagine what the world would be like if every trouble and squabble were carried over and added to from day to day without the leaven of forgiveness? The awful weight of human woe, hate, and condemnation very soon would annihilate all life and its expression. So, you see, forgiveness is not just a nice little act—it is necessary to the survival of humanity.

Let's consider this on the scale of a single life. Imagine what your life would be like if you had never forgiven anything or been forgiven for anything wrong that occurred! It is not likely that the emotional structure of any person could support such a burden. But in spite of all the forgiveness that is displayed in the world, it is still not adequate. Most of us are much too sluggish at times as channels for the expression of this quality. Family rifts have existed for years when forgiveness would have restored harmony and the joyous unity of the family circle. Friendships that once meant mutual happiness have been severed for lack of forgiveness. Misunderstandings between partner and partner, or employer and employee, have existed to the disadvantage of all concerned, when forgiveness would have meant all-round prosperity.

This is why it is so important that we learn the craft of forgiveness. We need finesse in our ability to extend forgiveness freely and easily. Forgiveness is the quickest way to end trouble and to have peace and unity. A forgiving spirit is a unifying force. It can remove the barriers of separation between peoples and nations, and weld them together in peace and good will. This is something that legislation or military might cannot accomplish. To hate is to become an instrument of destruction. But to forgive is to maintain our grip on life.

A minister once said that if Jesus had not found it in His heart to say, "Father, forgive them," as He hung on the cross, there would have been no resurrection. I would agree with this. The magnanimous expression of forgiveness is often the prelude to great advances in one's life. Any person who is bound in any measure by a sense of injustice or harbors condemnation or unforgiveness cannot hope to live a transcendent life. And this is what we are all working for—to be able to transcend the things that are detrimental to the good and productive and satisfying life.

Frequently, we wait until there are dark clouds of trouble before we extend our forgiveness. I recall hearing a story once about three children in a family who had had a terrific brother-sister disagreement during the evening. They had gone to bed very unhappy with one another. Early in the morning the parents were aroused by the noise of a violent thunderstorm. Then they heard an unusual noise coming from the children's bedroom. When the parents called out to the children, to find what was going on, one little voice answered, "We're all in the closet forgiving each other." On an adult level, we must not wait until those storm clouds gather before extending forgiveness. To forgive another person immediately is to eliminate a small trouble before it becomes a violent storm.

Forgiveness is one of the most difficult acts in the spiritual repertoire that we can be called upon to perform. And the reason for this is that often the persons who have treated us in a shabby manner are ones whom we have been fond of and have had great faith in. It is not pleasant to be disappointed in a person who *had* displayed such qualities as integrity, friendship, loyalty, and love. But it is not easy, either, to carry a load of disappointment in our heart day after day. Such an emotional burden interferes with our health and with the orderly progress of our affairs.

When it comes to having to forgive another person more than once, this was most aptly covered by Jesus Christ. Do you remember the story? Peter had come to Jesus and asked: "Lord, how often shall my brother sin against me, and I forgive him? As many as seven times?" And Jesus replied, "I do not say to

you seven times, but seventy times seven."
The implication here is, of course, that we
should forgive another person indefinitely, if
necessary. That doesn't mean that we con-
done what he may be doing, but we see to it
that we harbor no unforgiveness within ourself concerning him. That way, we are not
destroying ourself with the malignant quality
of unforgiveness. And we are not contributing
to the spiritual degradation of the other
person.

Unforgiveness may well be called spiritual
murder! "Seventy times seven" you may well
encounter those who stumble in front of you.
They may knock you off your feet in their
intensity or preoccupation as they hurry
toward some self-set goal. They may even try
to take something that you consider to be
yours, if it will further their own progress.
That is, they may accept honor and credit and
praise that you have earned. Perhaps they
may intrude on friendships and cherished
relations and claim any number of things that
you value. If this should happen, ascendency
is called for. You must let the human self of

you so merge with the divine Self that your forgiveness is as natural with you as your breathing.

The ultimate objective in this is to become so spontaneously forgiving that you are not even aware of the need to forgive. Forgiveness must simply flow forth from you, impersonally, as warmth does from a stove.

In Unity we use the expression, "I behold the Christ in you." This is what we must do. We must let the divinity in ourself strike a compatible note with the divinity in the other person. Then forgiveness becomes a joy rather than an obligation.

In addition to learning the master craft of forgiveness, it is also necessary to develop the ability to feel forgiven. Many persons find it difficult to receive the forgiveness of others. Even though they are told and shown that they are forgiven, feelings of guilt stand as a barrier to accepting forgiveness. Often, in order to feel a genuine sense of repentance for something we have done, we feel that it is necessary to suffer for a while. But no person can *be* forgiven until he *feels* forgiven. And it is not necessary to spiritual growth to prolong a period of self-punishment. A sense of self-punishment affects the soul in much the same way that malnutrition affects the body. Self-punishment inhibits and impedes the growth and development of the soul.

Remember that God does not want us to suffer. If we have that notion, then we are still a victim of the belief in an old bogey of a god that men have created in the image of some tyrant. God is not a sadistic master—He is the Spirit of infinite love. As such, His forgiveness is immediate and complete. And as children of a God of love, we should, if we practice, become masters of the craft of forgiveness.

One of the best-known stories about forgiveness concerns the great artist Leonardo da Vinci. Da Vinci once had an enemy against whom he harbored a long-term grudge. It is said that, as he was painting "The Last Supper," he decided to get even with his enemy by painting his face as the face of Judas. But the ugliness of the deed so depressed him that when he tried to paint in the face of Jesus, da Vinci simply could not get into the right spirit for such a sacred task. The face of Jesus would not come out right for him. His vindictiveness not only ruined his happiness, it also blunted his skill. But when he sought out his enemy and forgave him, and painted out the insult, then he saw the face of Jesus in a dream. The dream is supposed to have occurred on the very night on which he had forgiven the man. Then he was able to paint a face of Jesus that is one of the glories of the art world.

The message of this incident is that not only does unforgiveness give us inward misery, and assault our physical makeup, it robs us of talents and skills. This is a terrible price to pay for the supposed privilege of holding a grudge, or bearing a burden of unforgiveness, even if it is borne secretly.

THE MASTER CRAFT OF
Thinking

Ralph Waldo Emerson said, "Man surrounds himself with the true images of himself." And then he went on to write something that gives us much food for thought: "Every spirit builds itself a house, and beyond its house a world, and beyond its world a heaven. Know then that the world exists for you. For you is the phenomenon perfect. What we are, that only can we see. All that Adam had, all that Caesar could, you have and can do. Adam called his house, heaven and earth; Caesar called his house, Rome; you perhaps call yours, a cobbler's trade; a hundred acres of ploughed land; or a scholar's garret. Yet line for line and point for point your dominion is as great as theirs, though without fine names. Build therefore your own world. As fast as you conform your life to the pure idea in your mind, that will unfold its great proportions."

All men are created free and equal, in that we are given the only tool with which we can really build our life. That tool is our thought. All of us have the same material with which to build. That material is divine substance, available to all alike through man's indwelling Spirit. One of the most important things we can know in life is that as our inner thought is, so will our outer life be. All the universe is made of divine substance, the invisible matter of Spirit that is responsible for all creation. For us, this divine substance takes shape in the mold our thoughts give it: "We think in secret, and it comes to pass; environment is but our looking glass."

Many people doubt the teaching concerning man that says, "As he [man] thinketh within himself, so is he." These people say that they have worked to change their thoughts, but that it has not changed their lives and affairs. In effect, they say that this *cannot* be done. But in observing these people, I have learned an important fact. It is this: The people who say it cannot be done are the people who do not really want to do it. They say, "I've tried it, and it cannot be done." But the truth of the matter is that their efforts have been superficial. They haven't really tried. Many persons endear themselves to conditions in their lives, even though those conditions represent great trial to them. How many persons have you known whose sicknesses have become conveniences for them? A person who is chronically ill almost always gets special considerations. Even though that person may go through the motions of trying to change his life by changing his thought, his heart is not in it.

So if you have a problem in your life that seems to be tenacious, that you are having difficulty in dealing with successfully, and you have come to the place where you say, "I can't," make sure that you are not really saying, "I don't want to." *The law of thought-*

29

reproduction is a law of life, and it will work for anyone who really wants to work it! The reason our thoughts are so significant and powerful in our life is that they are the means, the *only* means, through which we may establish direct communication with God.

Emmet Fox has some interesting thoughts: "Whatever your real conviction of yourself is, that is what you will demonstrate. Whatever enters into your life is but the material expression of some belief in your own mind. The kind of body you have, the kind of home you have, the kind of job you have, the kind of people you meet, are all conditioned by and correspond to the mental concepts you are holding. The Bible teaches that from beginning to end."

There is so much proof that eternal energy or creative force is molded by thought that no intelligent person can now deny it. There was a time in the early days of the metaphysical movement when this was thought of as some sort of crackpot philosophy. But no more. I have been called a crackpot a few times in my life, but I consider this a compliment. After all, it takes a crack in the pot to let a little light in. One of the great truths we need to learn is that God hid the whole world in our heart, so when any object or purpose is clearly held in thought, its manifestation in tangible and visible form is merely a question of time.

There is one fine and important point that must be considered here. It is this: Every person demonstrates situations and experiences in his life in accordance with the thought-molds he provides. But he does not always demonstrate them according to his *specific* thought-molds. Let me cite an example. A man whose wife had passed on left him with four motherless children, two of them newborn twins. For a time the man's sisters and other relatives helped him with the children. But after a time they had to attend to their own affairs. It was about this time that the man came to the Unity center. He was heavily burdened as the wage earner and sole parent. Quite naturally he wanted a wife and a mother for his children.

The man began to make a mental treasure map of the type of person he wanted to meet and marry. In a very brief time he felt that he had found such a person, and he asked us to pray that this woman would marry him. We did not pray this prayer, however, because it was not for us to say that this was the right person. You see, not only had he decided what the temperament of such a person should be; he had even decided what she should look like physically. It is not necessary to go into the details, but had he married this particular petite blonde, it would have been a grave mistake. We learned later that she was a "divorce artist," and had had five husbands previously. This man eventually did remarry— a heavyset brunette. She became a wonderful wife to him and mother to those children.

You see, when you hold an image in mind, you must be willing to be flexible with it. You may think that there is a specific thing you want, and every bit of human willfulness in you tells you that that is what you want. But if you can set aside a purely human desire, you may find that God is trying to tell you that He has something better in store for you.

Hold your mental image of what you want from life, but hold it with a light touch. Perhaps God has a surprise for you. It may be as different in detail from what you think you want as that brunette was from the blonde. What the man really wanted was a good wife and mother. God took care of the details a little differently from what the man thought they should be, but it all turned out right. Nonetheless, you are molding your tomorrows. If you stick tenaciously with some mental image that is dictated by your human willfulness, whether or not it is for your highest good, you'll get it. And getting it may be the saddest thing that ever happened to you.

I want to give you five suggestions that you may use in utilizing the master craft of thinking, the formative power of your thought. First of all, you have to have the ability to dramatize yourself in your mind's eye. That is, not only can you image yourself as a whole, prosperous person, in the right em-

33

ployment, with the right friends, but you can actually image *situations* that would depict these attainments. Some people may call this daydreaming; but if it is, it is daydreaming with a purpose. I prefer to call it creative use of the imagination.

The second step is to prove your faith in your dream by making logical preparations for its fulfillment. As the kings of old did when they prayed for water and dug ditches, dig your ditches, prepare to receive the fulfillment of your dream.

Third, be willing to make adjustments in the minor details of this drama. The objective may remain, but always remind yourself that its fulfillment need not be according to your human specifications.

Fourth, be a finisher as well as a beginner. One job finished is worth a dozen half-finished. No horse ever wins a race if it does not go all the way around the track.

Fifth, keep your mental drama to yourself. Do not tell other people, as this only scatters your forces. Remember Samson? He could do anything as long as he kept his mouth shut.

Most people's minds are like boilers with the safety valve wide open. They never get enough of a head of steam to run their engines.

There is one blanket point that applies to all five of these steps. As each step is applied and worked at, this blanket point must be considered. And it is this: You must ask yourself, "Is all this really right, or is it just what I want personally?" *It has to be right, you know!*

We once had a very disturbing thing happen in a congregation of which I was a pastor. A man was going around town doing many questionable things. This man said he attended meetings at our center, but I did not know him personally. When the man was challenged about his actions, he said: "Unity teaches that I have freedom of thought. Also that whatever I think about, I may do." His justification for this was that the Unity teachings say it is all right.

That is *not* what Unity teaches! A person cannot do anything he wants to do in the name of free thought. Freedom of thought carries with it a tremendous responsibility. That responsibility is to see that our thought is as close to divine principle as our level of spiritual understanding enables it to be. That is the refining fire through which freedom of thought must pass.

Someone once said that there are three doors through which the words we speak must pass; they must not be said unless they may pass through all three doors. The same may be said of our thoughts. When you begin to plan your thoughts, ask yourself this: Is what I am about to think *kind?* Is it *constructive?* Is it *necessary?* If your thoughts can pass through these three gates, perhaps they are fit to be entertained in your mind.

One of the most exciting uses of the mind is with the imagination. It might well be said that the imagination, of all man's mental qualities, is the one that associates him most closely with God. The first mention we read of man in the Bible is where he is spoken of as an "image." "Let us make man in our image, after our likeness." The only place where an image can take place is in the mind, in the imagination. What this means is that man, the highest creation of God, is a creation of God's imagination. And God endowed man with an imagination of his own, so he too can employ the creativity of his mind.

The keynote to the successful use of man's faculty of visualization is this: We must see things as we think God wants them to be, instead of as they are. This we must do, of course, with the eye of the mind. Envisioning things as God would want them in our life enables us to put our life more closely in accord with the purpose of God for us. This is what everyone wants—whether or not he knows it. We may *think* we want what human willfulness dictates, but not really. What we *really* want is what God wants for us, because the will of God is always for the highest good of man.

One of the most successful approaches to alcoholism lies with using this technique: If the alcoholic can only envision himself in his deepest heart as the sober, responsible person he wants to be, he takes his greatest step in the direction of sobriety. This can be done in regard to any personal problem that may assault a person's life. The mental vision of the thing we want to attain is what sends us in the direction of that attainment.

One more thought about the master craft of thinking is of utmost importance, because it concerns the very salvation of the world. This is the thinking we ourself do about world conditions. The whole world is thinking about war: political war, economic war, and the war of armament. As long as we think of war, how can our dream of world peace ever be fulfilled? Here is a thought which puts the entire matter in focus, with the responsibility placed where it belongs: *"Let there be peace on earth, and let it begin with me."* If we owe anything to the survival of humanity, it is to find God's peace within ourself, and then to radiate that peace to the world. Peace begins with the Spirit of God within us. But it must be accepted in our own mind and thoughts, for we can only accept God's ideas of peace when our own thoughts are those of peace.

So the master craft of thinking is really that of *constructive* thinking. Until our thinking is divinely constructive, it is certainly something less than a master craft! Here is Paul's familiar formula for it: "Finally, brethren, whatever is true, whatever is honorable, whatever is just, whatever is pure, whatever is lovely, whatever is gracious, if there is any excellence, if there is anything worthy of praise, think about these things."

THE MASTER CRAFT OF
Prayer

It is important that we take a long, hard
look at the technique of prayer from time to
time . . . to make sure that we are using
prayer with effectiveness. Prayer is the most
powerful form of energy a person can gener-
ate. The influence of prayer on the human
mind and body is as demonstrable as are the
glands of the human body. Prayer is a force as
real as terrestrial gravity. It supplies us with a
steady flow of sustaining power in our daily
life. I suppose that we might say we really
never learn to pray until we realize that
prayer is a privilege rather than a necessary
duty.

To define prayer, we could say quite simply that it is the act of contacting God. And contacting God is very much like eating, in that no one else can do it for you. Others may inspire you to eat by preparing and serving delicious and attractive food. But if you are to gain the benefit of it, the actual consuming of the food is something you must do yourself. When it comes to praying, others may lead you to the portal of the experience, or they may inspire you to want to pray. But crossing the threshold into the actual experience of prayer is something each person must do for himself. One of the things I have observed and experienced over many years is that the quantity of the answer to prayer is always determined by the nature of the prayer itself. If a person wants big answers, he is going to have to pray big prayers.

For a person to learn to pray effectively, it is necessary that he learn where he must go to pray. It is not necessary that he go to some particular altar, or shrine, or magnificent church. Jesus gave explicit instructions as to where one must be when he prays in order to know the maximum effectiveness of prayer. He said: "And when you pray, you must not be like the hypocrites; for they love to stand and pray in the synagogues and at the street corners, that they may be seen by men. Truly, I say to you, they have their reward. But when you pray, go into your room and shut the door and pray to your Father who is in secret; and your Father who sees in secret will reward you."

Now, the reference to a "room" here does not mean a room in your house, but rather a room in your heart. Within every person is such an inner chamber. It is a sacred place. And this inner place is the sanctuary of prayer. Only when a person has journeyed within himself can he be sure that he is in the right place for a maximum prayer experience.

Part of the problem concerning prayer is that too many persons wait until they are in gross trouble before they resort to it. I once read a comment by a rustic philosopher to this effect: "Unless a man is in trouble, his prayers ain't got no suction." Factually, people do pray a lot harder when they are

43

faced with some challenging experience. In effect, they use God as something of a universal bondsman. When they get in bondage to some undesirable condition, they prayerfully "yell" for bail from God.

If this is one's only prayer practice, it is most unfortunate. As well as being communion with God, prayer ought also to be companionship with God. Through such companionship, severe trouble is eliminated from a person's life.

What many people call prayer is not really prayer. Just because a person starts out by addressing God does not mean that what is going to follow is real prayer. There have been times when someone has told me that he has prayed and prayed about some situation, but to no avail. When I have asked him how he has been praying, I find that what he calls prayer might more accurately be called "concentrated worry." He may start out by saying, "Dear Father-God," but what follows is a recitation of his troubles from a strongly negative point of view. When the so-called prayer time is over, more harm than good has been done. Why? Because the person has been devoting a definite period of time to concentration on his troubles.

Then there are those persons who feel that one must beseech God in order to get a favor from Him. This, it seems to me, is a contradiction. We have been told that we are children of God. But to have to beseech Him for an answer to our prayers makes us praying beggars. This is hardly in keeping with the way in which the child of a king ought to come before his heavenly Father.

A psychologist wanted to conduct an experiment. He hired a man to chop wood, and said to him, "I will pay you three dollars an hour, but I have only one request; you must use the *back* side of the axe." The hired man thought that the psychologist was a little strange; but the wages sounded good, so he took the job.

However, after working an hour and a half, the man knocked at the door. When asked what he wanted, he replied, "Mister, I'm quitting this job!"

"What's the matter?" asked the psychologist. "Don't you like the pay you're getting? If it isn't enough, I'll raise your wages."

"No," the man said, "the pay is good enough. It's just that when I chop wood, I've got to see chips fly."

Beseeching prayer is like chopping wood with the back side of an axe. If you want to see the spiritual chips fly, your technique and style of prayer must be constructive and affirmative.

There are also formal prayers, such as the ones we usually find printed in prayer books. But the whole essence of prayer, as it was taught by Jesus, is that is should be spontaneous and spring from the individual's heart. If someone has written out our prayers for us, and printed them in a book, then the backbone is sometimes gone out of them. This also goes for many formal prayers that are so stiff and wordy they sound more like literary readings than prayers. I recall an editor telling a story about when, as a boy, he went to the midweek prayer meetings at his church. At these meetings the people in the congregation were encouraged to stand up and pray aloud concerning their particular needs. The minister would also offer one of his grand prayers. This always seemed unfair to the editor, because the minister could think of so many more things to ask for. The editor said it was like a professional competing against amateurs.

Then there are the times when we have not clearly defined what we really are praying about. It is always well to be sure that we know what we want, so that we may be concise and well defined in our prayers. This, in turn, will get us a concise and well-defined answer. To show you how we get the wrong connotation to our prayers, let me tell you something I once heard. A little boy was told by his mother to pray that the weather would get warm and dry so that his grandmother's rheumatism would not act up. That night he said his regular prayers and then at the end he added, "Oh, yes, God, also please make it hot for grandma."

You see, it isn't that it is necessary *to God* that your prayers be well defined. It is important to *you*, because it is "according to your faith" that it is done to you.

Another question that arises with regard to prayer is: Does God ever say, "No"? Well, I can only tell you that I have lived to thank God that all the prayers I prayed were not answered in ways that I expected. Many times we pray in the fever of emotion or in the desperation of great need. Sometimes our prayers are not based on genuine need, but more upon the whim of the moment. Praying from the base of emotion rather than from reason, we often think we want things that we later change our mind about, after we have had time to consider those things more objectively. Perhaps God says "No" sometimes, but never without having said "Yes" to something better. The only time God says "No" is when we have prayed for something that is either too little or is not good for us. While He is saying "No" to such a prayer, He is automatically offering us something higher and better. For this reason it is wise to end every prayer we pray with the words, "This, Lord, or something better—if You will."

There are three fundamental ways that we

may pray. We may pray with our thoughts, with our words, and with our actions. To pray with our thoughts is to follow the instruction of Paul to "pray constantly." This means that we must always keep our thoughts on a high spiritual plane. If a person's sustained thought is prayerful, then he does indeed pray constantly. This in turn brings rich rewards, because a sustained prayer produces a sustained answer. It has been said: "We talk to God— that's prayer. God talks to us—that's inspiration." That sort of activity takes place in the mind. It is a mental conversation with God. The more constant the conversation is, the stronger our lines of communication with God are. Obviously, this brings a more exalted experience in life.

Most of us are familiar with the prayer of words, for it is this style of prayer that we use the most. But the mistake we make in this area is that we feel that only the words we speak during designated times of prayer have an effect on our life. We must not be misled here. Remember that Jesus said, "Men will render account for every careless word they utter." He also said, "By your words you will be justified, and by your words you will be condemned." Please note that the inference here is that *all* our words have an effect upon us. In spiritual consciousness the Master said, "The words that I have spoken to you are spirit and life." So we must know that all words are prayers, because they will produce an effect in our life in keeping with the nature of the words themselves.

Then there is the prayer of action. Perhaps this can be illustrated better than defined. A family in a rural community was in grave financial straits. A prayer meeting was called at the church so that the people of the congregation could pray for this family. During the meeting, while one of the deacons was offering a fervent prayer for blessings upon the family, there was a loud knock at the door of the prayer room. The door opened and there stood a sturdy boy. "What do you want, boy?" asked one of the elders. "Well," replied the boy: "Pa couldn't come to the meeting, so I brought his prayers in the wagon. Could someone come and help me please, and we'll bring them in?" Pa's "prayers" consisted of potatoes, flour, beef, turnips, apples, and jellies. Needless to say, the prayer meeting was quickly adjourned while a new approach to the problem was decided upon. This was praying with the hands as well as the heart!

There is an old saying that most of us have known from childhood: "God helps those who help themselves." Often it is necessary to put forth some real personal effort to bring about the answer to our prayer. Gladstone, the British statesman, told the story about a neighbor's little girl who really believed in prayer. Her brother had made a trap that caught sparrows, and she prayed that the trap would fail. One day her face became radiant, and for three days thereafter she prayed with such absolute faith that her mother asked her one morning, "Julia, why are you so sure that your prayers will be answered?" Julia smiled and replied, "I know that my prayer will be answered, because I went out there three days ago and kicked that trap to pieces." Would this indicate that her prayer had or had not been answered? It certainly was not answered *for* her, but it appears that it was indeed answered *through* her.

And that is another important thing to know about prayer. Our prayers are never answered *for* us. They must, by the very nature of creation itself, be answered *through* us. This means that any time we pray—by thought, word, or deed—that prayer places a responsibility on us. It is the responsibility to *be* the answer to our prayer. It means that somewhere in the evolution of the answer to the prayer, something is going to be required of us. But it does not mean that this responsibility should be a somber thing to contemplate. It should be a glorious thing to think about. After all, when a prayer is answered through us, we actually become an instrument of God. And what a glorious privilege that is! Surely the privilege of it far surpasses the weight of the responsibility.

The mechanics of prayer may be simply stated. They are *meditation, denial, affirmation,* and *silence.* The practice of these four steps is, of course, much more complex and involved.

MEDITATION is the act of getting yourself into the right frame of mind for prayer; that is, thinking about the things that will condition you to experience your prayer.

DENIAL is the act of cleansing from your mind and thoughts anything that would detract from the effectiveness of your prayer. This is the process by which you remove negation and destructiveness of thought.

AFFIRMATION is the act of decreeing for yourself the fulfillment of your prayers. This is the executive act of prayer in which you establish the nature and tone of what is to come to you. This step is based on the classic biblical passage, "You will decide on a matter, and it will be established for you."

SILENCE is the act of listening and feeling. This is the part of the prayer program that makes it a dialogue. In the previous steps you have stated your case, and you are now ready to wait silently for God's answer. Keep in mind that you can hear those answers only when you are silent. If your mind is filled with conflict, fear, hate, confusion, or any other negation, this mental static prohibits you from hearing God's answer. This is why silence must be a part of every prayer.

Perhaps of all the millions of things which have been said about prayer, the most significant was said by Jesus Himself. In these few words, He has given us the assurance that our prayers *shall* be answered:

"Your Father knows what you need before you ask him."

THE MASTER CRAFT OF
Prosperity

Most people are interested in being prosperous. The majority of us want the better things in life and feel that we are entitled to them. If someone were to ask you if you are ready to receive prosperity in your life, I am sure you would indicate that you *are* ready. But are you *really* ready for prosperity? It is hard to imagine not being ready and willing to welcome with open arms the good things we desire from life. Who wouldn't want to have a new car, the desired kind of house, a substantial pay raise, a promotion on the job?

But simply wanting material benefits does not mean we are ready for them. If we were, they would come to us. Make no mistake about it: the amount of prosperity we have at any given moment is the exact amount we are prepared to accept. To make room for more, we must go into training for it! We go into training for every other skill. To become a lawyer, dentist, doctor, engineer, nurse, or private secretary, one must put in a period of study and preparation. Painters, carpenters, plumbers, electricians, and mechanics serve an apprenticeship while they are learning their trades. The acquisition and proper handling of prosperity is no less a skill. Why should we think that prosperity is merely a matter of chance or luck, subject to no underlying laws of cause and effect? To attract a fortune (or even a small fraction of a fortune to meet a need), we need to learn the master craft of prosperity. And this craft is based on definite, spiritual laws—laws taught, demonstrated, and proved by Jesus.

Some people seem to be born with an innate understanding of the prosperity idea, and are able to apply its laws almost unconsciously. They use the prosperity idea intuitively, without even realizing that they are doing so. For example, one very wealthy and successful man was onced asked for the secret of his success. He replied: "It has just never occurred to me that I could possibly be poor. I expect money to come to me, and it does." Yet vast fortunes accumulated by men like this are often quickly dissipated by sons and daughters who are apparently untrained for prosperity. If a millionaire's understanding of the principles behind his acquisition of a fortune was unconscious, he cannot pass the understanding along to his children. So they soon come to grief when it is their turn to act as custodians of the trust.

Many persons who attract plenty are unable to keep it. With them it is "here today, gone tomorrow." Others, in various degrees of lack or want, seem incapable of attracting enough substance to meet their basic needs. In either case, what these persons require is not better luck but better training in the ground rules of prosperity, so that they can develop a true prosperity consciousness. It is all a matter of consciousness. With consciousness you attract prosperity, and with consciousness you keep it. If your consciousness is lacking, you either do not get the prosperity in the first place, or when you get it, you do not have it for long.

In his book *Prosperity*, Charles Fillmore makes an important statement in this regard: "You may think that you could live better and do more good if you had lots of money. Things would not be a bit better with you if you had a million dollars, unless you also had the understanding to use it for the good of yourself and others. . . . We must evolve with our possessions until we get the ability to handle them. Then the law is fulfilled."

Anyone who feels the financial pinch (and most of us do at times) wants to know how to be free from such situations. This brings us to the question of how we may be free from financial inadequacy. Well, how do we get free from anything? Jesus gave us the word: "You will know the truth, and the truth will make you free." But notice that there is a tremendous condition implied in this promise: you have to *know* the truth before the truth can make you free. Until you do that, you simply are not ready for the kind of prosperity that lasts, any more than you would be ready to solve a mathematical problem until you knew the tables of mathematics. If and when you know the truth about yourself, you will have every good thing you need. You will attract prosperity automatically. The truth about prosperity is simple, and can be stated in a few words, with three simple points:

God is the source of all prosperity. "Every good endowment and every perfect gift is from above, coming down from the Father of lights with whom there is no variation or shadow due to change."

There is no separation between you and God. "I and the Father are one."

God wants you to be prosperous and has already given you all that you can accept as belonging to you. "It is your Father's good pleasure to give you the kingdom."

All of this can be put into one simple statement, which affirms the truth that you must know in order to be free forever from lack and limitation: *God is my abundant supply.*

All that He has is mine and He wants to give it to me. I now claim my abundance of good. To claim your prosperity as already yours, not off in the future somewhere but here and now, is absolutely essential. Not to have this realization is like having money in your pocket and not knowing it. It is of no value to you.

Suppose that someone made a large deposit in a bank account under your name and for you, but didn't tell you about it. All the while your financial state was dire, and you didn't have enough to meet your needs. Of course, "ignorance is bliss," but if you were to find out about it later, it would be a frustrating experience. Yet this is precisely what life is all about. Because of the opulent nature of our creation and the fact that God has laid up vast treasures of ability within us, we now have an incredibly large balance in our spiritual bank account. But the majority of us do not know this. And until we realize the truth implied in the statement, it is not likely that we will be able to benefit from it. So get this statement firmly and clearly established in your consciousness: *God is my abundant supply. All that He has is mine and He wants to give it to me. I now claim my inheritance of good.* And remember that this is not just contemporary hearsay, but is based on biblical authority.

Properly understood, the Bible is a handbook of prosperity. Jesus dealt especially with the subject in His parables. A number of these parables give direct or indirect consideration to prosperity. The parable of the prodigal son dealt with the matter in a decisive way. There are a number of implications in this parable, but whatever else it talks about, it brings up the subject of whether or not a person can stray from the prosperity consciousness (the Father's house), and return again to receive its benefits. You remember that not only was the prodigal son permitted to return, but while he was still "afar off" from his father's home, the father went out to meet him. The boy was met with a lavish display of the signs of welcome. He was robed, a ring was put on his finger, and the fatted calf was prepared for a feast. Even if we have strayed from the prosperity consciousness, we can always learn (or relearn) the truth, and return to opulent living.

The elder brother of the prodigal son was jealous about the reception his brother received, and went away and sulked for a time. His heritage was waiting for him in the house, but he refused to take it. Many of us are like that. If you are continually comparing the amount of good others have to the amount you have, you too will probably feel unjustly treated. It is easy to feel that there is no justice, and that you have been slighted. But for one who has a prosperity consciousness, there is absolutely no justification for such an attitude.

There is another parable the Master told, about the laborers in the vineyard. The laborers were hired for different lengths of time during the day, but when they were paid, all received the same amount. The vital message in this parable is that we must not concern ourself with what other people are paid, regardless of how little or how much they work. In this parable, the householder met his contract with all his workers. And as long as our contract is being met by us and by our employer, we must not involve ourself in the affairs of others.

Jesus covered this tersely at another time, when He said: "What is that to you? Follow me!" In another parable, Jesus tells us to watch out for this attitude: "Why do you see the speck that is in your brother's eye, but do not notice the log that is in your own eye?"

There is one parable that we should read every time we feel any signs of self-righteousness in this respect. This is the one in which Jesus told of two men who went to the temple to pray, a Pharisee and a publican. The Pharisee prayed to God and gave thanks that he was not as the rest of men, extortioners and unjust, or even as the publican whom he saw praying nearby. But the publican prayed in the spirit of humility, asking only for mercy from God. Jesus made it clear that the publican's prayer was the more acceptable of the two: "Whoever exalts himself will be humbled, and whoever humbles himself will be exalted." The humble attitude is an important part of the prosperity consciousness, and of the truth you must know in order to be set free from all lack in your life.

Of all the stories Jesus told that dealt with the subject of prosperity, none dealt with it more decisively than the parable of the talents. This is a dramatic story about a man who was going to travel into a far country. Upon leaving, he called his servants to him and "entrusted to them his property." He gave five talents to one servant, two to another, and one to a third. Each servant was given the amount that his ability merited: "to each according to his ability." Each was instructed to see how he could increase the talents, and to give an account when the master of the household returned.

Upon his return a long time later, the master found that the servant with five talents had increased them to ten. The one with two talents was able to return four. But the one with the single talent could only return one, because in his fear he had buried his talent in the earth, instead of investing it for return. He met with the displeasure and wrath of his master, and was cast out into the darkness.

The obvious moral is that a person must be a good steward in the handling of whatever amount of prosperity he has in his life, be it little or much. When substance is well handled, it is increased. One statement in this story that is little understood (or much misunderstood) is: "For to every one who has will more be given, and he will have abundance; but from him who has not, even what he has will be taken away." In the light of understanding prosperity as a master craft, it becomes easy to understand this statement. You need only take the phrase "a prosperity consciousness" and insert it in two places: "For to every one who has [a prosperity consciousness] will more be given, and he will have abundance; but from him who has not [a prosperity consciousness], even what he has will be taken away."

There is an important principle implied in this parable: If a person uses the substance at hand in his life, he will find it a source of blessing. Remember what the master said to each of the two successful servants in the parable: "Well done, good and faithful servant."

THE MASTER CRAFT OF
Victory

Palm Sunday marks a most unusual event in the life of Jesus. Jesus was used to crowds. Spiritually starved, they followed Him about to hear the depth and wisdom of His teaching. At times the multitudes numbered in the thousands as they came to have their souls fed with His words. He taught: "Man shall not live by bread alone, but by every word that proceeds from the mouth of God." He was the supreme spokesman for God, and His words were nourishment for the souls of all who were privileged to hear Him. When Jesus taught in doctrine and in parable, there was always a gentle humility about Him. As I read

67

the accounts of His teachings at such times, I get the feeling that, although His teachings were forceful, Jesus was almost retiring in His role as a teacher.

But on the day we call Palm Sunday, it was different. Apparently Jesus had another message to convey. And He conveyed it by example rather than by His conventional method of teaching. All of this may have begun to take shape in His mind some weeks before. But the actual drama itself began on a hill, the Mount of Olives, that rises to the east of Jerusalem. At the foot of this hill is the Garden of Gethsemane, where Jesus prayed so fervently.

The actual drama of Palm Sunday began on the slopes of the Mount of Olives. The first thing Jesus did was send two of His disciples to the village of Bethphage, where they were to find "an ass tied, and a colt with her." They were instructed to bring the animals to Jesus. If anyone should challenge them for loosing and taking these animals, they were simply to say, "The Lord has need of them."

So the animals were brought to Jesus, and

68

some clothing was put across their backs. Jesus then mounted the ass and thus began this strange procession from the mount to the city. Apparently the people began to realize the drama of the situation and the excitement began to rise. We read that "most of the crowd spread their garments in the road, and others cut branches from the trees and spread them on the road." In addition to those who followed, many went before, waving palm branches and setting up a great shout. It was a shout that has rung now for twenty centuries. It seems to get louder and clearer with each passing year: "Hosanna to the Son of David! Blessed is he who comes in the name of the Lord! Hosanna in the highest!"

What was to follow is known as Jesus' triumphal entry into the city of Jerusalem. This included the casting out of the money-changers and the sellers of the sacrificial doves from the great Temple of Herod. The Master said: "It is written, 'My house shall be called a house of prayer'; but you make it a den of robbers." It is also written: "The blind and the lame came to him in the temple, and he healed them." A memorable week followed, the week that Ernest C. Wilson has called *The Week That Changed the World.* But for our purposes, let us consider just the part of the story outlined.

What was it that Jesus was demonstrating on this occasion? Part of it was no doubt the fulfillment of the ancient prophecy concerning the coming of the Messiah: "Tell the daughter of Zion, Behold, your king is coming to you, humble, and mounted on an ass, and on a colt, the foal of an ass." Surely some of the actions of Jesus were designed to fulfill the prophecy, but there was more significance than this to what He said and did. So we must acknowledge greater importance to this triumphal journey on Palm Sunday than just the fulfillment of a prophecy.

We read that Jesus came humbly, or meekly, as He rode the ass into the Holy City. But we must remember that one who is meek and humble is not easily angered and has a mild, patient, merciful, and compassionate disposition. So the fact that He entered meekly into the city does not mean that He entered weakly. The meek are the mighty, for they know that their strength stems from the inexhaustible divine Spirit within them.

I think the reason Jesus chose to make this triumphal entry as He did was that He felt the time had come to demonstrate the true stature of man—that man is indeed the product of a divine Parent. As such, man has within him all the ingredients for victory. If those ingredients are brought together in right measure, the results are "individual mastery." Jesus' example—mounted upon a lowly beast, moving in the midst of shouts of glory—was designed to hail the victorious spirit of man. Here, by example, He was demonstrating what He had previously taught: "He who is in you is greater than he who is in the world."

On this occasion, there is no record of anything Jesus might have said as He rode from the Mount of Olives, down into the Kidron Valley, and up through the gates of Jerusalem. Instead of speaking, He let His example be a teaching in itself. However, as we think about some of the things He previously had taught by word and incorporate them into this magnificent example of Palm Sunday, we are able to come forth with a program for our own spirit of victory. It is herein that the teachings of Jesus have their value. If they are regarded as having historical value only and not as being applicable to our times, then it would be a waste of time for us to consider them. But His teachings *have* a contemporary value. Properly applied, they enable us to rise triumphant over the lower forces of our life— the lower forces being represented by the animal upon which Jesus rode.

What is about to be shared with you is not something you have never heard before. It is a part of the heritage of our faith. It is a proved formula, and if it is followed implicitly, you are guaranteed that the gift of victory will be stirred up within you. This in turn will do two major things for you. First of all, it will enable you to transcend yourself and become a greater person than you now are. Second, it will enable you to achieve your highest good.

Although you may think it strange, the program for applying Jesus' teachings is based on something said by the apostle Paul, rather than by Jesus Himself. We all know Jesus' chosen disciples received their instructions directly by word of mouth. Much of what Paul received came by *inner revelation.* The communication between the spirit of Jesus and the spirit of Paul enabled Paul to gain great insight into things spiritual. You recall that his spiritual unfoldment began one memorable day on the road to Damascus.

Later, Paul compared life to the running of a race. The object of any race is to achieve victory by crossing the finish line ahead of all other contenders. In running the race we call "life," however, things are a bit different. We are not in competition with any other person to win the race of life. Our only competition is ourself. Victory becomes ours when we manifest our highest potential to such a degree that, in perfect honesty, we can say, "Today I am a better person than I was yesterday." This is the true transcendental experience.

The program is applicable in whatever area of life you may choose to apply it. In what area would you like to achieve victory? Is it in the field of business? in raising a family? in the action of being a good neighbor? in the conquering of a bad habit? in the art of finding joy in retirement? In what way do you desire to become a different person than you now are? Is it the expression of greater health? the manifestation of more supply? the building of a finer state of spiritual consciousness? Whatever it is that you seek, you can have it, if you now line up for the race—and if you pledge yourself to victory by following the simple program implied in these most beautiful words of Paul: "Brethren, I do not consider that I have made it my own; but one thing I do, forgetting what lies behind and straining forward to what lies ahead, I press on toward the goal for the prize of the upward call of God in Christ Jesus."

Do not take your desired good for granted. Paul says, "I do not consider that I have made it [the goal] my own." To put it another way, he could have said, "I have work to do." So do we all have work to do. We cannot sit back and merely assume that our good is going to fall into our lap by some mysterious means. Such an attitude is fatal! A runner cannot win a race if he takes victory for granted.

Concentrate on the single task at hand. "This one thing I do," spoke the apostle. The key word here is *one.* This emphasizes singleness of purpose, concentration on the "one thing" we seek to accomplish. Whether or not you know it, the one thing you want more than anything else is a greater awareness of the omnipresence of God. Spiritual consciousness is what it is called. How very much we need this reminder, because we are inclined to think that there are other things we desire more urgently! We dilute our powers to accomplish when we dissipate our thought-energies on a number of things at one time. Remember, the thought mechanism of the mind functions only on one track at a time. If you keep jumping the track, then by your actions you disqualify yourself and lose your opportunity for victory.

Release all past experience by not looking back. Paul states the importance of this step when he says, "Forgetting what lies behind."

Our past mistakes, failures, and feelings of inadequacy can only hinder our chances for victory and success at living today if we choose to gaze continually back upon them. A runner cannot be in a winning frame of mind if he looks back on the race he lost yesterday or last week. We cannot be in a winning frame of mind if we choose to look back on the limited person we appeared to be yesterday. It is just as important to develop a good forgettery as it is to develop a good memory—and perhaps even more so.

Strain forward toward your goal with all your energetic resources. Here are the apostle's words on this: "Straining forward to what lies ahead." Well, our *good* is before us. I do not mean to imply that our good is in some far distant place or dim future; but before us in the sense that, no matter how far we progress in life, lying just before us is the next treasure life holds for us. But in order to continue to be spiritually enriched, we must keep going forward—always moving in the direction of that unlimited good which God holds for us.

Remember that Paul wrote to the Corinthians, "What no eye has seen, nor ear heard, nor the heart of man conceived, what God has prepared for those who love him." Just as a runner reaches for the finish line, we must stretch our spiritual, mental, emotional, and physical muscles toward our goal. Such action expands our capacity to accomplish—and sustains us until we reach our goal.

Persist in keeping your inner vision upon the goal. "I press on toward the goal." These words of Paul imply absolute persistence in beholding our good. Whether the goal we pursue is visible or invisible to our physical sight, we must always keep our inner vision of it, no matter what. This keeps our mind from becoming "fuzzy" and our actions from losing purpose. The runner who does not persist in the vision of victory, even while he is running, does not achieve success.

One final commentary: The "prize of the upward call" offered by Paul is the achievement of our highest good in life. It is "the prize . . . of God in Christ Jesus." What is this prize, or highest calling, of God? It is to be a

Christlike person. It is to be commanded by compassion. It is to be motivated by meditation. It is to be propelled by prayer. It is to be cognizant of consciousness. It is to "run with perseverance the race that is set before us." It is to transcend our lower self. It is to learn the master craft of victory.

THE MASTER CRAFT OF
Love

Let us consider the quality that is the most refined spiritual attribute that man has: the quality of love. In its spiritual expression, love makes of man a god. But when it is misrepresented, it turns him into a very devil. Love, properly expressed, has been responsible for some of the most beautiful accomplishments in the world. But when it has been improperly expressed, it is responsible for misdirected acts that cause unhappiness. Of all the teachings of Jesus, none is more direct and far-reaching than what He taught about love. But even though He taught directly and simply, many persons are unable to understand the implications of what He said concerning love.

Let us delve into this quality of love, to see if we can get more insight into what it is really all about. In understanding love, we may apply it to benefit ourself and the lives we touch. In her book "Shadows on the Rock," Willa Cather made this rather provocative observation: "Sometimes a neighbor whom we have disliked a lifetime for his arrogance and conceit lets fall a single commonplace remark that shows us another side, another man, really; a man uncertain, and puzzled, and in the dark like ourselves."

Probably all of us have had the experience of having to deal with or live with someone whom we feel we just don't like. If you have never had this experience, you are a rare and fortunate person. Because all people are different and we are thrown into the company of all kinds, somehow we have to work out a system of learning to love these people—even if we do not like what they represent. You may think that it is impossible to love some people because of the way they behave. But actually, there is a way of dealing with other people that has little to do with what they are or what they do. This is a system that does not depend on good results for a reward.

The best way to get along with people is to love them. The greatest human need in the world is for love. This is not only what people need, but it is what they want and what they respond to. However, demonstrating such love is not always easy. At least, it is not easy at first—until one develops his ability along this line.

It is generally understood that we are supposed to love everyone. But this idea is not taken seriously by most people. We all have our likes and dislikes among people. The injunction to love everyone is viewed by many of us as (at best) an impossible ideal, and (at worst) sentimental twaddle. So, before any of the following suggestions are going to work for *you*, you must make up your mind that you are going to give them an honest try.

We are all aware that there are people in the world who do hateful things, and seem not the least bit sorry for what they have done. There are people who are just plain boring and unattractive. These are some of the people toward whom we have no inclination to express love. I am sure that Jesus was aware of this very thing when He said: "Love your neighbor as yourself," and, "A new commandment I give to you, that you love one another." Now, remember that Jesus was a realist at all times. He did not profess ideals that were beyond the reach of human attainment. Rather, what He taught was designed to call forth the best that is in man—to enable man to call up divine reserves that in turn enable him to transcend his mere humanity.

In order to understand what Jesus understood about man, we have to become quite definitive about this word *love.* It is a rather fuzzy word in the English language. In Greek, the language in which the New Testament was written, there are three variations for the word *love,* each having a different meaning: *eros, philia,* and *agape.*

The word *eros* means being drawn to another person because of his attractiveness; that is, the object of the love is, in itself, the source of the love. The most complete fulfillment of such love may be found in a happy marital relationship. But a person may quite properly feel such love in varying degrees toward any number of persons. It rests in the beauty, charm, merits, or talents of the person so loved.

The second type of love, *philia*, is the friendly, fraternal type. Two persons are often drawn together because of some mutual interest or concern they may have. Liking the same things, they are attracted to each other. This form of love can sometimes be sad. You find it in a marriage where the husband and wife no longer have true love for each other. But they stay married because of their home or some other mutual concern or interest.

With the *agape* type of love, we find something quite unlike the other two kinds. It does not depend upon the attractiveness of another person or upon shared interests. This type of love arises from recognition of the need of the other person for love, for interest, and for fellowship. This type of love has no "angle," it does not insist on its own way. This is the kind of love that is implied when we are commanded to love not only our neighbor but our enemy.

To give the sharpest definition possible to *agape*, Jesus chooses an example in which no elements of *eros* or *philia* are intermingled. He says, "Love your enemies and pray for those who persecute [hate] you." Quite humanly and naturally, you will feel negative, rather than positive, in your emotional response toward those who are "against you" or have tried to harm you. It will be difficult to feel a sense of sharing toward those who seem to detest you. But this does not mean that you cannot help your enemy out of a difficult situation, feed him when he is hungry, offer him companionship when he is lonely. And this is the sort of activity that is called for in this very spiritual expression of love.

Since none of us is yet expressing the Christ consciousness in all of its fullness, our own time and resources are limited. Those persons to whom we are bound by ties of love and mutual interest usually have first priority. This is what Paul might have had in mind when he wrote, "Let us do good to all men, and especially to those who are of the household of faith." In other words, there are those who would seem to get our special interest. Yet if the goodness we show is limited to these only, we are not really displaying the kind of love Jesus was talking about.

When Jesus commanded, "Love your neighbor as yourself," there was a lawyer who asked Him, "And who is my neighbor?" Jesus did not give the man a definite answer. Rather, He told him the story of the good Samaritan. You know, in those times the Samaritans and the Jews would have nothing to do with one another. It was a feud that had been going on for five hundred years. But in the story, a Samaritan saw a Jew lying injured by thieves along the side of the road, and he helped him and saw that he was cared for. That is, he responded to a need.

There is an important consideration here. Day after day, our paths cross those of people in need: an unattractive girl working at our office; a man at a party who is withdrawn and self-conscious; a fellow worker who feels insecure in his job and needs to be encouraged. There are just a few of the opportunities that are presented to us almost daily—opportunities to respond to a need. It may not always be convenient to respond to these needs, anymore than it was convenient for the good Samaritan to interrupt his journey and take care of the wounded man. But he responded to the need. And if we are to learn the craft of love, we must respond in like manner. The situations to which we respond may not be as dramatic as the one in the parable, but the need may be just as urgent.

You recall that, in this story told by Jesus, a priest and a Levite came down that same road, but they avoided the need and crossed to the other side of the road. They probably felt entirely justified in doing this. After all, this was not their affair, so why should they interfere? We hear about this same sort of thing today when, in large cities, people have needed help while being attacked, and others stood by and watched. They didn't do anything about it, because they didn't want to get involved. Interestingly enough, these people feel just as justified as did the priest and the Levite. But love means involvement. Spiritual love means compassionate involvement where there is a need to be met.

If you have love in your heart, this automatically means that you must have some rapport with all people. You cannot be indifferent. Involvement is love. And oftentimes the grandest expression of love is toward people from whom there is no possibility of response. We must not extend some act of love toward a person, expecting that it be returned. We must love because we have the spirit of love within us. And it is our spiritual nature to extend love.

Let me illustrate the difference between human love and spiritual love. Human love has its origin in one person and its fulfillment in another. That is, human love, coming from one person, must have another person toward whom that love is directed. When it is received by the other person, it is fulfilled. But spiritual love has its origin in the divine Spirit within us, and its fulfillment in expression. You see, this spiritual love wells up within us, and we just express it. It doesn't have to be directed toward any one person. Spiritual love is simply and impersonally expressed. It may be received by anyone who comes within its aura of influence; anyone for whom it may meet a need. Human love is often narrow and confined, while spiritual love is free and sweeping.

I am sure you have heard the old cliché, "If you are nice to people, they'll be nice to you." Well, there are at least three things wrong with that cliché. First, it may be true some of the time, but it is untrue enough of the time to result in cynicism. We often hear this cynicism expressed: "I've learned not to go out of my way to help people. They never appreciate you; people just use you." Second, to give out in the hope of getting something back is a selfish quality of love. It is not at all what Jesus had in mind. Pure *agape* is the love that gives with no expectation of return. We cannot remind ourself of this too often. Third, when we do good in the hope of changing an attitude toward us or of gaining some advantage, the nature of the act is "writ-

88

ten all over us." People will know what we are doing. Everyone is sensitive to love with an "angle."

There is another approach to this idea that is most unsatisfactory. Some people do good turns for others they do not really care for, not because of the others' needs, but because it builds up their own ego. This in turn poses additional difficulties. First of all, selfish love is unjustified. You see, all of the time, means, and talents with which we may do good are not really ours. They are God's—on loan to us. We are obligated to use a spiritually borrowed talent in a spiritual way. This is a matter of divine ethics. Second, self-righteousness creates an intolerable twist in the personality, which makes us much less effective in our relations with others. So the act of expressing love has to be done right. If we give love its proper expression, our life unfolds like a beautiful flower. If we withhold it, we wither on the vine.

I do not mean to imply that the adequate expression of love needs to be complicated. On the contrary, it is most often adequately expressed in the simplest and most common-place aspects of life. For the most part, we do not need to go outside our family or our neighborhood to begin to find opportunities to express love in a spiritual way.

The nature of the craft of love is to love, because it is our nature to love. We are created in the image and likeness of love. And love, spiritually expressed, is not concerned with the worthiness of the recipient. We just love because we must.

THE MASTER CRAFT OF
Calmness

Calmness is one of the crying needs of our contemporary world. Because of the nature and tempo of life in our modern society, the quest for calmness is one of the most urgent pursuits of man. And perhaps this is the great paradox of our times. We pursue with urgency a quality which (by its very nature) must have no sense of urgency incorporated in it.

The quest for calmness is not a new thing. Rather, it is one that has endured through many generations. For example, one of the oldest blessings that men have given to each other is "Peace be to you." This blessing is found in several books of the Bible and variations of it appear in many other books. Then we also have promises of peace and calmness. Isaiah said: "Thou dost keep him in perfect peace, whose mind is stayed on thee." And the Master promised: "Peace I leave with you; my peace I give to you; not as the world gives do I give to you."

Somehow we have had difficulty grasping this sense of inward peace. Yet to have it is essential to the living of the spiritual life. No person in inward turmoil can hope to be in satisfactory personal communication with God. Thus it is that personal calmness has become a rare quality in human life. We must come to realize the character of this most important spiritual attribute. Calmness is the poise of a great nature, in harmony with itself and its ideals. It is the moral atmosphere of a life which is centered in God, and is self-reliant and self-controlled. It is singleness of purpose and absolute confidence and conscious power—ready to be focused in an instant to meet any crisis-situation.

There are a number of different types of persons who "appear" to be calm. But the quality of their calmness is certainly not high enough to be called a master craft.

One type might be called the "sphinx type," typified by the Great Sphinx of Egypt. But a statuesque individual who is unmoved by all feeling does not typify true calmness, because inaction is not calmness; it is a death, the silencing of all the energies. True calmness has a vitality about it. No one lives his life more fully, more intensely, and more consciously than the person who is really calm.

Then there is the "fatalist type" of person, who appears calm. But the fatalist is not truly calm. Rather, he is resigned. He is often the coward-slave of his environment. He hopelessly surrenders to his present condition and is recklessly indifferent to his future. He accepts life as a rudderless ship, drifting on the ocean of time. He has no compass, no chart, no known port to which he is sailing. His self-confessed inferiority to all nature is reflected in his attitude of constant surrender. This is not calmness. This is resignation, and there is a vast difference between the two.

The man who is calm has his course in life

clearly marked. His hand is always on the helm. He has a spiritually based calmness and does not have to worry about the rough seas in life, because he knows that he is equipped to handle them.

Such a person knows that, should some stormy situation arise in his life, he has a choice of reaction. He can exercise the divine authority which has been given him. Following the example of Jesus, he can declare to the rough sea: "Peace! Be still!" Or he can ride out the storm, secure in the knowledge that in the center of cool calmness within him he has the resources to face life in a four-square, victorious manner. This is the same sort of confidence displayed by Jesus in facing the experience of Calvary. He was confident in the secret knowledge of His overcoming victory and resurrection.

The truly serene person knows that the source of his calmness is within. He does not try to purchase it across the prescription counter. He knows that in the deep part of himself is a wellspring of peace, and that that peace is untouched by life's surface winds.

When there is a great storm at sea, only a relatively shallow depth of the sea is affected. Down deep, the sea is always calm, regardless of how intense the surface winds may be. Man is like a deep sea, if only he knows it. He is privileged to seek refuge from the assaults of life by journeying into the deep and serene part of himself. Also, he may project his inner serenity into his outer countenance. Then he will find that calmness is the crown of self-control.

While personal serenity and calmness in themselves represent an achievement of great stature, there are other extra dividends that come with these qualities. These are what give majesty to calmness. One of these dividends greatly to be desired and much pursued is that of wholeness—not only physical wholeness, but wholeness in every aspect of man's being. A calm mind has a profound, regenerative, and hygienic influence upon our well-being.

In 1759, John Wesley wrote a rather interesting item in his "Journal." He told of a woman who had a continuous pain in her abdomen that failed to respond to medical treatment. He found that the pain resulted from what he called "the woman's fretting over the death of her son." John Wesley then observed that when she was comforted by religion, the pain disappeared. This caused him to ask the question, "Why then do not all physicians consider how bodily disorders are caused or influenced by the mind?" This was more than two hundred years ago, yet this is precisely the idea that physicians are considering in our time.

Dr. Wilson G. Smilie, professor of public health and preventive medicine at Cornell University Medical College in New York, once told the American College of Surgeons that not only are there no known remedies for most of the degenerative diseases—those of aging which affect the heart and arteries—but "there are not likely to be any until doctors begin preventive measures that involve man's social and economic condition as a probable starting place for these diseases." In other words, the worry and fear indulged in by persons who are confused and bewildered by insecurity in our rapidly changing world bring about degeneration of their vital organs. Now, obviously, if a mind plagued with the turmoil of worry and anxiety can degenerate a person's body, then a mind blessed with the serenity of peace and calmness can regenerate it. The glory of calmness itself is manifested as glorious wholeness in the body.

During World War II certain flyers became convinced that they would be nauseated and sick at high altitudes. Flight surgeons believed that much of this sickness was induced mentally by the fear of altitude. So they developed a flight chamber in which all of the conditions of flying could be simulated. Then, when some new pilot complained of such sickness, he was put in this flight pressure chamber. At what the pilot thought was pressure adjusted to 17,000 feet (but was actually equal to that of about 3,000 feet), he became ill. But when the pilot thought the pressure was adjusted to 3,000 feet (when actually the pressure was that of 17,000 feet), he felt normal again. This was evidence that the problem was not at all physical; just the symptom was physical. The problem was in the area of the psychoneurotic, and the treatment was then confined to that area. The result of treating the cause instead of the symptom was remarkable. When the pilot was conditioned to take a calm mental approach to the altitude, he no longer became ill.

There is a growing list of what we might call "man-made" diseases, and a recent candidate to this list is arthritis. This is the conclusion of famed neurologist Stanley Cobb, of the Harvard Medical School. Dr. Cobb has stated that in the treatment of arthritis, the main cause is still an "X factor"—unknown. But he and his associates have reported in the Journal of American Medicine that "poverty, grief, and family worry" are closely connected with the swollen knuckles and aching of rheumatoid arthritis. In the Massachusetts General Hospital, fifty arthritis patients were interviewed by a psychiatrist or social worker, who asked them to talk freely of their early life, family relations, work, marriage, children. Dr. Cobb reported that in all but seven cases, there seemed to be a definite relation between their troubles and the arthritis. Interestingly enough, in twenty-one of the cases, the worry and the arthritis began about the same time.

The human stomach has long been known to be a most accurate reflector of the attitudes. There is an interesting case recorded, which proves this beyond any shadow of doubt. In a book titled "Human Gastric Function," two doctors, Stewart Wolf and Harold G. Wolff of the New York City Hospital, tell about a shy, proud little man, known in the book as Tom. When Tom was nine years old, he drank some extremely hot soup that burned (and finally closed) his esophagus. For more than forty years he fed himself through an opening that surgeons had made in his abdominal wall. This enabled the doctors to peer directly into his stomach and watch carefully what happened to the human stomach under varying conditions.

A great part of the value of the doctors' findings lies in the fact that it is a record of the stomach's color, secretion, and activity when the patient is relaxed and feeling secure, as well as when he is full, hungry, worried, and angry. When an officious secretary made Tom so angry that his face got red, so did his stomach. Anger, worry, or fear caused a greatly increased flow of acid secretion—whether or not there was food to be digested in the stomach. We know that stomach ulcers are provoked by excess acid, and so these doctors came to the obvious conclusion that such stomach disorders are best treated through the proper management of personality problems. This, of course, is just another way of saying "thought control." Once again, if an anxious, worried, angered mind produces ulcers, then it is obvious that a calm, serene, peaceful mind can be the only permanently effective help.

One more ailment that is a candidate on this list is the condition called colitis. For years it had been thought that colitis, which is an inflammation of the colon, was caused by the invasion of some pathogenic organism. But so many cases of this did not respond to prescribed treatment that another consideration had to be given to it. According to one medical dictionary: "In the most common forms of colitis no disease-producing germs have been identified, and, in fact, there is good reason to believe that none will ever be found, and that the condition is 'functional.' A functional disease is one which is not produced by organisms or agents introduced from outside, and in which the stimuli producing the disease arise within the body, generally from some part of the nervous system." If a mind troubled with adverse emotions can cause difficulty, then the opposite effect would come from a calm and serene mind; that is, out of calmness comes wholeness.

There is now substantial evidence that most accidents are traced directly to upset emotions. Dr. Herbert J. Stack, director of the New York University Center for Safety Education, has compiled a record of hundreds of cases in which accidents stemmed from anger, grief, and fear. He brought out this interesting point: An "extreme" emotion makes a dangerous companion in the driver's seat. This pertains even to such emotions as extreme joy. But a feeling of calmness and serenity gives a person the necessary control of his faculties that makes him much less prone toward having an accident of any kind. So, you see, a lack of emotional control can be costly and unhealthy. But when our emotions are calm and controlled, they are conducive to a most enjoyable life experience. A quiet mind and emotional maturity constitute the greatest treasures in life. The reason for their value is, of course, that they have an important and constructive transforming effect upon us.

This is not just a new concept of modern, psychological science. This is a centuries-old concept and an integrated part of the Christian teaching. In his letter to the Romans Paul said, "Be transformed by the renewal of your mind." In his writings to the Philippians, he gave a sound, valid formula (referred to in a previous chapter) as to how a person must think in order to have a peaceful transformation in his life: "Whatever is true, whatever is honorable, whatever is just, whatever is pure, whatever is lovely, whatever is gracious . . . think about these things. . . . And

THE MASTER CRAFT OF
Marriage

Marriage has been with us for a long time, for it has been an institution of the Christian faith since the beginning of Christianity. Let us keep this in mind: marriage is much more than an institution. It is an adventure; it is a career; it is an enterprise; it is a fine craft; it is a school for the development of virtues. Because of its very intimacy, marriage, more than any other human relationship, can bring out the best in people or the worst. It can and often does mold inexperienced, undisciplined young people into unselfish, kind, responsible citizens. On the other hand, it can turn two normal human beings into cynical, discontented, and contentious members of society.

With some of the obvious, human limitations we seem to have, a certain amount of tension becomes evident from time to time in just about every marriage. Often, there is not too much we can do about the tensions themselves. But there is a great deal we can do about how we handle and react to them. If we are aware that these tensions may crop up from time to time in marriage, and govern our reactions accordingly, we can avoid a great deal of the unhappiness that plagues many marriages. Some people, however, will not take this viewpoint. They feel that marriage is always going to be a golden mist. This results in their making demands on marriage that the institution of marriage was never designed to fulfill.

There are people who go into marriage expecting the worst, and they usually get it. That's the way the law of life works. But those who expect the worst are a minority compared to those who make unreasonable demands on marriage. They set their expectations of each other not on the basis of having married a human being, but rather on the basis of highly idealized, unreal images. They match their mate and their marriage against these images. Whenever one does this, both the mate and the marriage often seem lacking.

Too many married persons keep their eyes wide open, closely observing to see if their mate is measuring up to the ideal and the dream that they held in their heart. When things are not measuring up to the ideal, they become resentful and dissatisfied. Then they begin to look for an escape through the divorce laws. Or they stay together, making each other miserable by holding to fantasies of how wonderful it might have been had they married someone else. I have observed that, when a marriage begins to deteriorate, one of the most important things a couple can do is seek professional counseling. This is available through many religious and social agencies in most cities.

Often when couples find that the "lilt" has gone out of their marriage, they look back and ask: "What has happened? Where did it go wrong? We were in love—ready to share, give, and sacrifice. Each other's happiness seemed the most important. There were the dreams of a home and children. Why didn't it continue that way? What happened?"

Well, it would be wonderful if marriage could work out just as smoothly and as free from tension as the hopeful and starry-eyed newlyweds want it to. But the record shows that often it does not. Perhaps we go about it in a wrong way.

A cultured Oriental man was visiting in the United States. He was asked about the difference between marriage in America and in his country. This was his answer: "In China, marriage is like a cool teakettle on a hot stove; after a time it comes to a boil. Here, it is like a hot teakettle on a cold stove. After a time it cools off." There is much to think about in these words.

There are some factors to be considered with regard to reactions and overcomings in marriage. One of these is: Don't hide your feelings! One of the most obvious, yet least recognized, of the tension-producing factors is the mere state of being together day after

108

day, week after week, month after month for twenty, thirty, or forty years. Two human beings, no matter how sweet-tempered, no matter how deeply in love, cannot be together for all this time without having some tensions build up occasionally.

Certainly people in love want to be together. But they also want and need to be alone at times. Yet how many husbands will chance hurting their wives by saying: "Look, honey, I'd like to go off by myself for a day or two, just to be alone. It isn't that I don't love you—I just want to be alone." How many wives would chance offending their husbands with the same kind of request?

Sometimes this yearning thrusts itself to the surface, but before it can be expressed it is choked back, leaving a bitter mouthful of annoyance and resentment. Then, instead of a person making a request such as that, in a kind, intelligent fashion, harsh and hurtful words are spoken.

Some people labor under the delusion that in marriage they have given up something more precious than what they received, namely their freedom. If that feeling becomes pronounced, it is an aggravating element. If they are honest with themselves, most people will have to admit that the pleasures and advantages they have gained through marriage far outweigh the advantages they might have retained by staying single. But just knowing this does not always deal effectively with the yearning to be free again to go where they want to go and do what they want to do. When the urge arises to break loose, trying to squelch these feelings is not the answer. Oftentimes that only makes the harness chafe even more.

When such feelings are repressed, conflicts and frustrations build up within us. But instead of just throwing up our arms and shouting, "Give me liberty or give me death," many of us begin to get these frustrations out of our system by picking on our spouse about little, meaningless things, such as leaving the cap off the toothpaste or hanging a jacket on a doorknob. And the thoughts we have within us eat away at our good nature.

It seems to me that a frank and understanding discussion of these feelings between the persons involved is a strengthening factor in marriage, because it removes many of the cankering, little irritations that weaken the structure of an otherwise fine marriage. When marriage partners cannot talk these things over with each other, this is the time for a third party to be brought into the picture to counsel the couple.

Through adequate marriage counseling, any marriage can be helped. And premarital counseling is also a valuable experience. Many times through such counseling in preparation for marriage, a couple finds that there are many things they do not understand about each other. Premarital counseling enables those involved to deal with these things reasonably. But if differences come up after marriage, they are often dealt with emotionally instead.

In some marriages, difficulty arises because of differences in temperaments. These differences are inevitable, and they are necessary, if we are to retain and further develop our individuality. When two people marry, they are not supposed to give up their individuality. Every person needs to retain some of the qualities that make him a person. By developing more similarities than differences, the balance will be in favor of a happy marriage.

But remember that these similarities are not handed to us on a platter. They must be worked out and developed as mutual interests. Some people like to read; some like to talk. Some like a lot of social activities; some are quiet homebodies. Some like spicy foods; some prefer their food bland. These are differences, of course. But if some similarities are cultivated to offset them, they are not detrimental to the marriage.

There is no sure way of ascertaining in advance precisely how a person is going to act after marriage. Usually we can get some idea based on the person's habits and behavior. This is not always conclusive, however, because through the years we all change. Sometimes we hear a woman say that she has been married to the same man for fifty years. This is ridiculous. It is a good bet that she has had an entirely different type of man every ten years. And this is true of the wife as well.

I know this is so in my marriage. Just about the time I get my wife figured out, she is ready for a new step in growth, and I have to start all over again. People are like ice floes, with the portion hidden below the surface greater by far than that portion which shows. But I think that adds flavor to marriage. Look at all the surprises it offers!

A person ought to bear in mind that when he gets married, he does not get a "brand-new" product. After all, the person who marries has been in the process of development for twenty, thirty, or more years. During those years he has developed a whole assortment of special needs, cravings, and expectations that are going to demand some measure of fulfillment in marriage.

Marriage is a composite of little acts of love and sacrifice. It succeeds when both husband and wife agree on certain basic principles in advance. Small grains of sand can either go into the making of a firm foundation, or they can become abrasives. The same is true with

113

the little acts of marriage. If a person just knows this, he can do much to avoid changing an ideal into an ordeal.

Christopher Morley once said, "The plural of spouse is spice." Well, spice is a piquant seasoning. And some of the most tasteful seasoning you can put into a marriage lies in a few well-chosen words, spoken at just the right time. These are the grace notes in the symphony of life.

In the famous Church in the Wildwood, a brief ceremony has been added to the wedding ritual itself. As the newlyweds leave the chapel, the pastor tells the bride that it is the tradition for her to ring the church bell. It is fixed, however, so that the bride cannot ring the heavy bell by herself. Then the pastor motions to the bridegroom to help her. As the bell rings, the clergyman says: "Bear in mind that marriage is much like the bell rope. It is much easier when you pull together."

Marriages may be *made* in heaven. But *people* have the responsibility for their successful maintenance!

114

THE MASTER CRAFT OF
Courage

One of the great needs in the world today is courage. War, international tensions, national crisis, and crime run rampant. The daily headlines scream with stories of grave personal, political, and social unrest. It takes a decided inward fortitude to live comfortably in today's world. Everyone needs to develop on his own behalf the master craft of courage.

That doesn't mean that everything is wrong with the world. There is a lot right with it. But we cannot live in a "fool's paradise" and close our eyes to those things that need changing and that represent a danger to us.

Of course, this is not to say that danger is

the exclusive property of the twentieth century. Much to the contrary, it has been here since the beginning of time. But our vital concern need not lie with the dangers men have known in the *past*. And our only concern with the *future* should be to make the best possible preparation for it in the *present*. We are concerned with evolving the right quality of courage to meet victoriously the challenges of today's world—the one in which we live. And we cannot deny that the dangers that are with us in our time are significant.

In "Henry V" Shakespeare wrote this thought: ". . . 'Tis true that we are in great danger; The greater therefore should our courage be." So, whatever else our time is, it is a time when men should stand tall and express a magnitude of courage that befits the magnitude of the challenge. Worry and fear caused by war and uncertain world conditions, as well as uncertainty concerning the future, have eaten like acids into the marrow of mankind. No responsible adult has escaped the tidal wave of concern that sweeps over the world today.

Worry is debilitating. Fear paralyzes the springs of action. The need for a remedy that will release soul and body from the grip of the twin evils of worry and fear is a paramount need of our day. And that remedy lies with the iron virtue of courage. Courage is the magic alchemy that transforms a person. Courage enables us to surmount difficulties, to rise up on the ladder of challenge, and to turn obstacles into stepping-stones. With courage, the thinnest armor takes on double thickness and strength.

It was Emerson who said, "What a new face courage puts on everything!" Of all the qualities of character that provoke the admiration of men, there are few that do so with such spontaneity and universality as does courage. This quality of courage makes an appeal to something deep in human nature, which neither friend nor foe can resist. We may not always agree with the cause for which a man stands courageous. But usually we all stand in admiration of the courage itself. We live in a time when fashions and modes of conduct have changed drastically. But courage is never outmoded. The appeal of true courage in meeting the issues of life is timeless, changeless, and universal.

Courage may be said to be the foundation for all the other virtues. Sir James Barrie once said, "All goes, if courage goes." And a similar conviction was held by Samuel Johnson. He observed of courage, "Unless a man has that virtue, he has no security for preserving any other."

The Biblical calls to courage are many: "Be of good courage." "Be strong and of good courage." "Be strong and very courageous." "Deal courageously." "He shall stir up his power and his courage." These are just a few of literally dozens of such references to courage. They tell men to take heart and have faith in God, and thus to know courage in meeting the issues of life.

Some virtues are like spring flowers that come for a season and then perish before the onset of cold weather. But courage is more like a perennial that shoots its blossoms, not only amidst the soft zephyrs of May, but also in the blustery winds of December. Courage has blossomed in every season of the race's history, and knows no limitation of border or race. No one people has a monopoly on it; it is the heritage of all. The fatherland of courage is all the earth, and all men are its potential heirs.

Although it is a quality that is highly prized by all men in all lands, I do not think we can say that courage has been a common virtue. Unfortunately, and from a human point of view, courage is not a common virtue. The feet of many persons are weighted with the lead of fear. It was Benjamin Franklin who once gave this somewhat negative appraisal of men: "Mankind are dastardly when they meet with opposition." But even though courage has not been a common virtue, this does not mean that it cannot be. All men have within them the divine Source of courage. And when we learn how to draw upon this inner reserve, we shall find that we have more courage to express than we had ever dreamed.

The kind of courage of which all men are capable was demonstrated in the life of our great Way-Shower, Jesus Christ. He had the courage to associate with the Samaritans, who were despised by the rest of the Jews. He knew that in doing this He would invite the wrath of His countrymen. He spoke courageously at the synagogue at Nazareth—so courageously that He was driven from the town. His courage was flashing when He matched wits with the scribes and the Pharisees. Before Pilate He stood as a tower of courage. And the courage He displayed at the time of His crucifixion is immortal.

Since the role that Jesus played on earth was that of a Way-Shower, the example of His life gives us some insight into the kind of courage each of us is capable of displaying. Jesus Christ was not the only one created in the image and likeness of God. The very core of His message was to inform all men of their own divine potential. This means that all of us have reserves of courage within—courage that springs from the very Spirit of God.

But remember that courage is never to be confused with recklessness. Courage must have eyes, as well as hands and feet; it must be courage that first measures the magnitude of a challenge, and then takes effective means to cope with it. Along this line, it was Fenelon who said, "Courage is a virtue only as far as it is directed by prudence." Joanna Baillie states this case well also:

> "The brave man is not he who feels no fear,
> For that were stupid and irrational;
> But he, whose noble soul its fear subdues,
> And bravely dares the danger nature shrinks from."

Courage and fear are not opposites. Courage does not mean the absence of fear, but its subordination.

Men who have done some of the most courageous deeds of history have confessed to being greatly afraid. One example of this was Napoleon. It is said that one morning at Waterloo, Napoleon's knees trembled so badly that he had difficulty climbing into his saddle. Looking down rather contemptuously at his shaking knees, he is said to have shouted: "Shake away, knees! You would shake worse than that if you knew where I was going to take you." That day five horses were shot out from under him. But the story of his courage is history. It wasn't the fact that he did not know fear, but that he was able to subordinate it. And that is courage in action.

Of course, few of us are ever called upon to display courage as valor upon a battlefield. And we pray that the time will come when no man will have to do that. Rather, most of us are called upon to be courageous in meeting the everyday challenges of life. Frequently these are more difficult than meeting some outward and more dramatic situation. This is because the everyday issues of life are often so subtle. A dramatic battlefield experience is usually brief and is over in a matter of hours or days. But some of life's experiences last for years, and keep pecking away at us. This calls for sustained courage.

The moment many people open their eyes in the morning, they are faced with another full day of finding the courage to keep on. Then they must frequently reach even deeper within themselves and find more courage to keep on keeping on. But the heartening message of the Christ tells us that sufficient courage to do this is available to us. I would say that most people have no idea how much courage they have at their disposal. Consequently, very few people ever live as courageously as they are capable of doing.

We should also remind ourself that there is a certain cheerfulness inherent in courage. Life is filled with occasions that challenge our courage and our fortitude. As I have mentioned, these are often the everyday things. That is, they are the prosaic and the homely tasks of life. And the divine expression of courage through us enables us not only to do these things of the everyday variety, but to do them with a joyous serenity. There ought always to be a note of cheerfulness in the things we do in the name of courage. After all, courage is a divine attribute. And when we are expressing courage, we are expressing divinity. This means that at such times we are actually "bearing witness to God." To bear witness to God is one of the rare privileges of life, and we ought to have an underlying joy when such a privilege befalls us.

Sir Phillip Sidney, many years ago,

expressed this same thought with regard to the gallant knights of his time. He said, "A true knight is full of gay bravery in the midst of danger." A similar observation was made by Emerson: "And that which takes my fancy most in the heroic class is the good humor and hilarity they exhibit."

Not less than seven times in the Old Testament do we find the admonition, "Be of good courage." In the first Book of Chronicles, Joab says, "Be of good courage, and let us play the man for our people, and for the cities of our God; and may the Lord do what seems good to him." The implication here is that when men are courageous, there is always a divine Ally. Joab was telling his people that if they would do their best, God would be with them to accomplish what was right in His sight.

And isn't this what we are all looking for in life? We want that which is right in the sight of God to prevail in our life. In order to have this, we must do our best in living, and our divine Ally will see that His order prevails for us. I think this is the same ideal Abraham

Lincoln had in mind when he made the noble declaration, "God and one constitute a majority." The Psalmist expresses the same conviction that divine aid will not be lacking for the man of courage who places his trust in God. His counsel is: "Wait for the Lord; be strong, and let your heart take courage."

Herein lies the secret of courage. It is this inner confidence that God is at our side that brings a smile to our courage. It is this knowingness that binds us to be of good cheer as we go forth to meet the challenges of life. When we have this knowledge of Truth, we know that God *is* on our side. And with God on our side, nothing can harm us. No one could possibly rob us of the ultimate victory of successful living. When we are reinforced with the realization of a divine Ally, we are able to face whatever is presented to us in life with a sense of confidence and joy. We are able, as the poet puts it, to "greet the unseen with a cheer."

Saint Teresa once wrote a few lines of verse to serve as a bookmark. This bookmark has now become quite famous, and it would be well to memorize these words:

"Let naught disturb thee,
   Naught fright thee ever;
All things are passing,
   God changeth never.
Patience e'er conquers;
   With God for thine own
Thou nothing dost lack—
   He sufficeth alone."

What the sun is to vegetative life, God is to the courage in the hearts of men. Place a board on your lawn and deprive the grass of the benefit of the sun's rays, and it will soon wither and die, for the sun is the source of its energy and sustaining vitality. Remove the consciousness of God from the minds of men and the well-spring of their courage and joyous serenity will speedily dry up.

But if you will constantly remind yourself that the Spirit of God within you is the source of your courage, you will know that, since God is from everlasting to everlasting, your flow of courage can never diminish. You are the vehicle for the very courage of God to be expressed. Knowing this, how *dare* any of us ever become discouraged? To permit ourself to become discouraged is a sacrilege. It betrays our purpose for being.

THE MASTER CRAFT OF
Happiness

In about 35 B.C., the poet-satirist Horace asked quite a piercing question: "Is it by riches or by virtue that men are made happy?" The interesting thing about this question is that men are still trying to answer it. Many people in this world feel that true happiness lies in riches. They feel that happiness lies in the accumulation of money and things. Unfortunately, many of them find that they are still not happy after they have their accumulation of riches. This does not mean that a rich person cannot be happy. But it does mean that a truly happy person has a consciousness of happiness, unrelated to things.

129

If we say that a consciousness of happiness is a virtue (and it certainly seems to be), then there ought to be no question as to whether it is "by riches or by virtue that men are made happy." Someone once said, "The picture of happiness is in the frame of mind." So true! This means that we must see to it that the frame of mind is of such quality that it truly encloses, or embraces, the state of happiness. And when we speak of the quality of the "frame of mind," we are talking about the quality of consciousness.

The thoughts that I want to share with you here are thoughts that are designed to help you develop such a quality of consciousness. Then you will know true happiness, because it will spring from the deep part of your self—deep where joy is a part of your heritage.

There are some people who think that it is a spiritual sign to be gloomy. I don't think this is true. Nor do I think that Jesus was a somber individual, as He is often depicted. You will recall that He was the kind of man who liked to eat with His friends. He attended at least one wedding party we know of. He loved the laughter and gaiety of little children. I get the feeling when I read the Gospel accounts of His life and works that He was the kind of fellow who loved life. And anyone who loves life has to be happy in his approach to it. Not only was Jesus' approach one that was seasoned with joy, but He taught that others should live happily and with joy: "These things I have spoken to you, that my joy may be in you, and that your joy may be full." Jesus was a man with a great zest for living, and with a keen appetite for the love and joy of life.

Granted, we live in a world that sometimes offers much to detract from our happiness. But being morose will not help the situation any. Modern man is inclined to take life far too seriously, which may well be the reason why his world is full of troubles. The importance of humor and joy should never be forgotten. A sense of humor changes the quality and character of our entire cultural life. There is purifying power in laughter—both for individuals and for nations. If they have a sense of humor, people are keyed to good sense, clear thinking, and a peaceable temper.

I have observed that pious people often use their piety as an excuse for dullness. Those who do this do a great disservice to their religion. They make it seem as if heaven is a place filled with intolerable bores. I say that religiosity without charm or humor creates more rebels than converts. God cannot be a Spirit of solemnity, or He would not have blessed man with the incalculable gift of laughter. The idea that having fun is against God's will does not ring true. The God who made giraffes, a baby's fingernails, a puppy's tail, a crook-necked squash, and a young girl's giggle has to have a sense of humor. Make no mistake about that!

I wonder if you have ever thought of this strange fact. Of all the countless people who have lived on this planet since its beginning, I have never read in history (or in legend) that anyone ever died of laughter. Much to the contrary, we are told in the Bible: "A cheerful heart is a good medicine." Indeed, life pays a bonus to those who learn that happiness is a vital part of living. It is one of God's

132

richest gifts. The Lord loves a cheerful giver, but He also loves the cheerful—and so does everyone else!

We must learn to find happiness wherever we are, and in whatever particular state of affairs we find ourself. Too many people postpone their happiness by thinking that it will come later, when something is achieved or acquired. But this is not good, as the consciousness of postponement keeps our good and its attendant happiness somewhere in the future.

To illustrate this, let me relate a story I once read. It was told by William L. Stidger of the theological school of Boston University. One of his students was walking down a steep hill in Boston one day shortly after a snowfall, and saw a youngster skiing with one ski. He stopped beside the boy and said, "Son, don't you know that you are supposed to have two skis?" The lad looked up with a happy grin and replied: "I know I ought to have two, but I ain't got 'em. But, mister, you can have a lot of fun with one ski, if you ain't got two."

The Book of Proverbs makes mention a number of times of the constructive effect of joy. After stating, "A cheerful heart is a good medicine," the writer continues, "but a downcast spirit dries up the bones." So if a person is sorrowful of heart, his spirit dries up; and, in turn, conditions the person for negative experiences, even illness.

Not only will a consciousness of happiness enable a person to escape this possibility of negation; it will also open the door for a truly opulent experience of life. Along this line, also written in Proverbs is the saying:

"All the days of the afflicted are evil,

but a cheerful heart has a continual feast."

As we have grown up, most of us have learned the rules of proper physical living but not the rules of proper metaphysical living. *Metaphysical* simply means living above the physical, or living in the spiritual. We have learned how to dress and eat and read and write. We know how to function reasonably well in earning our daily bread. But so many of us have *not* learned the important lesson of controlling our emotions. Yet in the control of our emotions lies the key to happiness.

The one single, most-important act in emotion-control is *prayer*. Let us assume that you do take time for such prayer. With this assumption, I want to share with you a program of seven brief suggestions. If you follow them, you will gain the emotional control that will in turn give you inner joy. This joy will open the door for you to a more effective and opulent experience of life.

"Accentuate the positive and practice cheerfulness." During World War II, we used to sing a song that carried a message along this line. Most of us sang it lightly, but its message is an important one. This ability to accentuate the positive is one that must be practiced. Anyone can do this, if he really wants to and is willing to put forth the effort to do so.

Paul was in prison when he wrote, "Rejoice in the Lord always; again I will say, Rejoice." In other words, display happiness even when your circumstances seem to be other than happy. How do we do this? Just a little further on, Paul tells us: "Finally, brethren, whatever is true, whatever is honorable, whatever is just, whatever is pure, whatever is lovely, whatever is gracious, if there is any excellence, if there is anything worthy of praise, think about these things."

The second point is, *don't cry over spilled milk*. Some people are continually thinking over, brooding over, and talking over every defeat, setback, or frustration they can think of. Any person who lives in the negative past is going to make himself miserable. This, in turn, is going to make him unhappy.

What do we do about this? Let us once again take our instruction from Paul: "Forgetting what lies behind and straining forward to what lies ahead, I press on toward the goal for the prize of the upward call of God in Christ Jesus." This means that if you are inclined toward living in the negative past, you should turn your attention toward spiritual things. Think of how you can be of greater service to the fellow members of our great human family. This will get your mind off yourself. We all need to quit worrying about the past, and to stop indulging in self-pity. If we stop crying over spilled milk, we shall be much happier.

Avoid unnecessary bickering and arguments. Life is just too short to spend it in arguing, bickering, and backbiting. Many times this is nothing other than a bad habit. Anyone can learn to use tact and diplomacy in dealing with others, if there is a disagreement. Bickering and arguing can be as destructive as the plague. No one ought to degrade himself as a child of God by lowering himself to such a thing. In the Old Testament Book of Job the question is asked, "What doth your arguing reprove? (A.V.)" You wouldn't go around deliberately hitting yourself on the head with a hammer, would you? Why do anything deliberately that is even more harmful?

Learn to turn your defeats into victory. Obviously, if a person acts defeated by every little setback in life, he is not going to be very happy. But if he makes up his mind that there is a lesson to be learned from every experience, then learns it, he is better equipped for meeting similar experiences in the future. This means that he has turned his supposed defeat into victory. This applies to major setbacks as well as to minor ones. Sometimes the bigger the setback, the more important the lesson is to learn. There is a New Testament passage from I Corinthians that says, "Thanks be to God who gives us the victory." The person whose mind is spiritually inclined is the one who tends toward victory. And this surely is conducive to greater happiness.

Face and handle your problems with big-mindedness. To have a big mind means not engaging in mental pettiness. Do not "fly off the handle" quickly. Temper control is a major contributor to a person's happiness. If you make up your mind to approach and handle each challenge in life calmly and without loss of temper, you will find yourself endowed with a mighty power to control your life. Listen to this:

"He who is slow to anger is better than the mighty,
and he who rules his spirit than he who takes a city."

Build faith in God. When you are confronted with the aspects of life that tend to detract from your happiness, you sometimes need all the help you can get. And what is the greatest help you can get? "God is our refuge and strength, a very present help in trouble." If you believe in God as a very present help, rather than a distant, reluctant Being, you will find that your faith in such a God will serve to help you meet the issues of life with courage. When you meet life courageously, you usually meet it successfully. When you feel successful at living, you are a happy person. This is why faith in God is so important to being happy.

Finally, be a doer. There is no use knowing about how to live more happily if you do not do something about what you know. This is why Jesus was so emphatic when He said, "If you know these things, blessed are you if you do them." And in the Book of Romans, we find this thought: "It is not the hearers of the law who are righteous before God, but the doers of the law who will be justified." Most people know the things they ought to be doing in order to promote greater happiness in their life. The problem is not so much one of not knowing as one of not doing. If you will *do*—you will be happy.

What, after all is said, is happiness? It is a greatly to be desired quality of life. It is the life described by the Master: "I came that they might have life, and have it abundantly." *Abundant life!* This is happiness. And remember that the abundant life promised by Jesus is not a promise to be fulfilled in some future heaven. Rather, it is to be fulfilled here and now. This is to bring forth the kingdom of heaven on earth. And, "If you know these things, blessed are you if you do them."

THE MASTER CRAFT OF
Repentance

The subject of repentance is one that is not discussed too extensively. Perhaps this is because, by its nature, it seems to have negative undertones. Yet repentance has a definite place in an individual's attainment of peace. Since all of us are searching for an abiding inner peace, repentance does take on importance. Webster says that to repent is to amend one's life. Or as one man puts it, "Repentance is being so sorry for sin that you quit sinning." We may be able to add amplifying sentences that involve technical words and phrases, but it is doubtful that we can improve the definition.

141

What repentance actually amounts to is the individual's awaking to the cause of his short-coming (or sin, as it may be called), then taking some definite action to amend the cause of it. Conviction is not repentance. It is one thing to awake at five o'clock in the morning, and it is quite another thing to get up, to act.

I suppose that the great classic example of repentance is that of Paul. As Saul, he was a professional religionist among the Jews, and he persecuted the early Christians. Then one day on the road to Damascus, Saul had an inner awakening. So pronounced was the real-ization of the significance and beauty of the work of Jesus Christ that dawned on Saul that everything about him was eventually changed. Saul became Paul.

Paul had repented, and he wanted to amend his life in which he had played the role of the persecutor of good men. It has been said, "If a man once gets a good look at Jesus Christ, he will never be the same man again." Surely this was true of Saul of Tarsus. From the moment the Christ was revealed to Saul on the Damascus road, to the time of his departure from this world, he led a new life. His life became a dramatization of his own words: "If any one is in Christ, he is a new creation; the old has passed away, behold, the new has come."

In a sense, then, repentance is individual conversion, and is designated by a "repaired" life. There is a vague idea that repentance implies sackcloth and ashes, but when we remember that Paul says, "All have sinned and fall short of the glory of God," we begin to realize that repenting of one's sins, or errors, is a necessary step in soul unfoldment. In fact, its importance cannot be overemphasized. Jesus said, "Unless you repent you will . . . perish."

In the material world we are accustomed to terms such as "useful arts" and "fine arts." By useful arts we mean the technical skills necessary to maintain a comfortable world. Man must have some sort of protection for his body: shelter, clothing, and food. These represent the fruits of the useful arts. We understand fine arts to mean the artistic skills

143

that enhance life. Art, music, literature, fruits of the mind represent the fine arts and provide satisfaction for the aesthetic nature of man.

In our endeavor to grow spiritually we discover shades or degrees of repentance that promote soul growth which might be likened to the useful or the fine arts. A person may repent of what is called a cardinal sin— murder, theft, and the like. Repentance for such acts is absolutely necessary if one is to enjoy any sort of mental, emotional, or physical health. We may repent of thoughts and words and acts that we feel are hindering our progress, that are peculiar to us as individuals and that no one but we ourself can know or understand. This is surely a fine art.

Repentance is a composite of many different feelings. All true repentance carries with it a feeling of sorrow or regret for having failed to measure up to the potential goodness inherent in our soul. Sometimes the feeling becomes extreme—arriving at heartbreaking degrees of guilt. Of course some persons feel the need for repentance more keenly than others, even though their errors may not be very serious. Man may choose his own time to repent his errors (or to amend his thinking and living), but eventually, we are told, "Every knee shall bow, every tongue shall swear."

Today all over the world many persons are choosing to repent their errors, though they may be unaware of their real state of mind. There is a great worldwide spiritual recovery in process today. Meditation is replacing the use of drugs in the lives of many of our young adults. People are turning to God in search of the important things in life—health, harmony, and prosperity. They are seeking peace of body, mind, and affairs through penitence.

Even though the world sometimes seems beyond repair, we must never forget the love of God for His creation. Jesus demonstrated God's love and good will for all men through the magnificent charity and compassion that He displayed in God's name. He came to feed the hungry, heal the sick, open the eyes of the blind, unstop the ears of the deaf, cause the lame to walk and the dumb to speak, and raise the dead to life.

Perhaps we are not hungry or sick, and so we may feel out of harmony with these urgent aspects of the ministry of Jesus Christ. But no person's heart is totally free of discord. And the message of Jesus Christ also taught how the love of God can remove discord between man and man, to bring peace, harmony, and freedom into his life. But divine love can find major activity within a person only when that person has cleansed himself through genuine repentance.

Certain religions of the world teach that one's errors (or sins) accumulate as a weight or burden on one's soul. This is called karma, which must be worked out of the soul through a number of incarnations—until the soul finally attains a perfect unity with the Creator. This is a notion that has served man, and has probably brought consolation to many persons down through the centuries. However, it has been found to be a hindrance to the swift development of man's soul, and it has been supplanted by a vastly different idea in the teachings and works of Jesus Christ.

146

The Christian religion differs in that it teaches that Spirit transcends time, and that man may receive his desired blessings *now*.

In the story of the paralyzed man whose four friends carried him on his bed to Jesus, we have one of the most convincing examples on record of the power of God to forgive man's sins instantly. The healing of the physical body was the blessing that all five men had in mind, but instead of healing the man's body immediately and letting him go, Jesus used the occasion to call attention to the divine idea of the instant forgiveness of sins. "When Jesus saw their faith, he said to the paralytic, 'My son, your sins are forgiven.'"

Learned scribes and Pharisees, men well versed in the beliefs prevalent among the Jews, were in the audience listening to Jesus that night. While the paralyzed man still lay on his bed, these men debated among themselves the statement that had been made by Jesus, saying: "Why does this man speak thus? It is blasphemy! Who can forgive sins but God alone?"

We quickly perceive here that Jesus did not resent these men's honest questionings. His claim was an unusual one, and He made it in the face of age-old beliefs that gripped His people in the clutches of hopelessness and despair. He was no doubt aware that these men had heard of His power to heal the ills of the physical body. Now He would have the occasion to reason with them about His power to forgive man's sins instantly. So He asked them: "Which is easier, to say to the paralytic, 'Your sins are forgiven' or to say, 'Rise . . . and walk'?" Then He continued by saying: " 'But that you may know that the Son of man has authority on earth to forgive sins'—he said to the paralytic—'I say to you, arise, take up your pallet and go home.' And he rose and immediately took up the pallet and went out before them all; so that they were all amazed and glorified God, saying, 'We never saw anything like this!' " In their amazement even the learned scholars were now convinced that they had witnessed a new teaching and work, whereby the forgiveness of sins was possible here on earth. And as written, they too glorified God.

No doubt you have been in churches where people have testified that their sins were forgiven at a particular day and hour. Surely the paralyzed man could have recounted such an experience. However, a definite feeling that our sins have been forgiven is sometimes difficult to come by. More often our experience is like that of a child growing up and beginning to understand by degrees that he was born into and is a member of a certain family. Even though we may not be consciously aware that our repentance has been followed immediately by a feeling of the forgiving love of God, we know that the promise is true: "If we confess our sins, he is faithful and just, and will forgive our sins." This is something that can happen now, not in some nebulous hereafter.

There was the woman who bathed the feet of Jesus with her tears. Of her the Master said, "Her sins, which are many, are forgiven." Obviously we do not always immediately accept forgiveness for our error, even as we do not always accept our health or our pros-

149

perity immediately, and the fact that we may need to repent rather often should not deter us from repenting and seeking a sense of forgiveness again and again.

When Peter asked Jesus: "How often shall my brother sin against me, and I forgive him? As many as seven times?" Jesus allowed for our possible repeated transgressions and our need for sustained repentance by replying, "I do not say to you seven times, but seventy times seven." How much more then will God forgive us if we turn to Him in repentance! Surely not many of us stand in need of forgiveness more than 490 times a day. But even if we should, then we need only remember the great promise: "My grace is sufficient for you."

As regards past errors, we must learn not to torture ourself with their memory. You recall that Jesus said, "Let the day's own trouble be sufficient for the day." Repentance held long in consciousness ravages the soul. It destroys initiative, the determination to keep on trying. Remember that the pardon of God comes quickly and thoroughly to the repentant heart. But that pardon must be accepted before it can be of any value to us.

One of man's great difficulties lies in his inability to forget his errors after he has done all that he can to make amends for them. Once the lesson has been learned, then the error must be released, as it no longer serves a constructive purpose. Bear in mind the promises that God will forgive our iniquity, and that He will remember our sins no more. If God is willing to forget our errors, does it not stand to reason that we should also?

John the Baptist commanded the Pharisees and the Sadducees to "bear fruits that befit repentance." In other words, let us bring forth results appropriate to our repentance, results that will insure peace and harmony for us. Instead of doubting our ability to regain and retain peace and tranquillity after we have repented, we must affirm our faith in a living God who is able not only to forgive our errors but to free us from committing them again.

Then things change: in situations where before we used hate, we now use love; for fear, we substitute understanding; for despair, hope; for stubbornness, patience; for gluttony, temperance; for turbulence, peace; and for sadness, joy. With all of it comes the assurance that some day there will be nothing in our world to mar its beautiful sublimity.

It is related that Michelangelo once stood before a great block of marble that had been rejected by some builders and cast aside. As he stood there with eyes staring straight at the marble, a friend approached and asked what he was looking at. "An angel," came the reply. Michelangelo saw what the mallet, the chisel, and patient skill could do with the rejected stone. He set to work and produced one of his masterpieces.

This is how God looks upon and sees possibilities in this chaotic, misshapen, and anxious world we live in. The time has long been ripe for us to give the divine Sculptor a chance to show what He can do.

THE MASTER CRAFT OF
Healing

The master craft of healing is something of a natural craft, conceived in sympathy and born of necessity. Men have sought strange and interesting ways to produce wholeness in their bodies. They learned very early in history that there were certain healing principles evident in nature. And they worked to devise methods of invoking them more fully, as well as of learning how to cooperate with these principles more effectively.

The physician, in one form or another, came upon the scene a long time ago. During Egypt's zenith, three thousand years ago, medicine was so highly organized that specialization had begun. Herodotus, the Greek historian, wrote this about the Egyptians: "Medicine is practiced among them on a plan of separation; each physician treats a single disorder, and no more: thus the country swarms with medical practitioners." So, we can see that medical specialization is not something new, but is at least three thousand years old.

Whatever his role might have been, the physician was mentioned early in Bible times. We find this passage in the Ecclesiasticus of the Apocrypha: "Honour a physician with the honour due unto him ... for the Lord hath created him. For of the most High cometh healing, and he shall receive honour of the king. The skill of the physician shall lift up his head: and in the sight of great men he shall be in admiration."

In the very early development of the craft of healing, the most primitive approaches to healing were mental. In those early days of man's existence, it was believed that sickness was owing to the invasion of the body by evil spirits. The witch doctor came upon the scene

154

with incantations, which were designed to drive out these evil spirits. In some cases this method worked, and actually produced healing results. These early witch doctors were shrewd observers, and they also began to note that certain herbs seemed to possess medicinal properties. Powdered or brewed into an infusion, the herbs could be applied to the exterior of the body for the healing of wounds and bruises, or taken internally for pains and other distresses. So witch doctors gradually added medications to their incantations. Since this knowledge was valuable to them, and enabled them to retain power in the tribe, they guarded it jealously, allowing no outsider to pry into the mystery of the treatment.

The witch doctors imparted their knowledge to their eldest sons—keeping it strictly in the family. In order to keep the treatment a secret, they surrounded it with an atmosphere of mystery. As time went on, the body of knowledge possessed by the witch doctors grew to remarkable proportions. But then specialization began. Some preferred the use of incantations, while others were inclined toward the use of medicinal herbs. Thus came the birth of two long-standing services, physicians and priests. Those who preferred the use of the herbs are the forerunners of today's physicians. Since the incantations eventually became prayers, those who preferred them later became the world's priests. We are all familiar with the advances that have come since those early times. Within the medical profession has been compiled a profound amount of knowledge and techniques for healing man's body.

Now let's go back nearly two thousand years and consider the life of another physician—Jesus Christ. In the historical account of the life of Jesus, we find repeated references to the fact that He healed people. He healed "every disease and every infirmity among the people." Some of the things that He did cannot be done through the advanced medical techniques of today. He could restore a withered arm to perfection in a matter of seconds. He healed people of leprosy simply by convincing them that they were clean. He restored the sight of blind people—some of whom had been blind from birth. He enabled the lame to walk again, not through orthopedic surgery but through faith and prayer. He even brought back to life again people who had died from their illnesses.

These works were done without the benefit of the surgery or medication of the modern physician. They were done through the power of faith. This means that there is a way through which a person can go directly to the Source of healing within him—to the divine healing principle—and activate that healing without the use of any outside agents. Jesus Christ proved so dramatically that this can be done that the world has stood in awe of Him ever since. But because many people have not understood that He worked with a universal healing principle, they have come to the unfortunate and erroneous conclusion that the healing abilities demonstrated by Jesus Christ were His and His alone. And they have worshiped Him because of these magnificent accomplishments.

But somehow, these people have overlooked some important items about the Great Physician. First of all, He never wanted people to worship Him. "Why do you call me good?" He asked. Second, He did want people to apply the things He applied in life. He said, "Follow me." And third, too many of us have overlooked an extremely important truth He gave in John 14:12: "Truly, truly, I say to you, he who believes in me will also do the works that I do; and greater works than these will he do."

This statement implies that the healing techniques used by Jesus Christ are available to be used by anyone who really wants to use them. Spiritually induced healing is a vital part of the religion of Christianity. Since the time of the personal ministry of Jesus, we have believed that He was chiefly concerned with the souls of men. Certainly, this was one area of His concern. But anyone who reads the gospel account of His life and accomplishments must come to realize that He was also vitally concerned with the bodies of people as well. He was interested in physical as well as spiritual welfare. This is proved through the repeated healings He performed. Interestingly, more people made direct appeals to Him for physical healing than for anything else.

Today we have built a great movement around the life of Jesus. Eight hundred million people profess to believe in Him and His works. But what has happened to this whole business of healing within the Christian church? Obviously, it has become obscured. We have become so involved in worshiping the Man that we have forgotten to follow Him in this area. He taught that the source of healing is God. He also told about the nature of God. But through the years we have completely misconstrued this teaching. He said, "God is Spirit." In saying this, He was telling us that there is a universal spirit or principle which, if used properly, will make men whole and keep them whole. But the theologians of the Christian era have beclouded the issue by declaring that God is in the shape of a man, ruling over a kingdom located somewhere out on the edge of the universe. This isn't at all what Jesus taught. You will recall that He said, "The kingdom of God is in the midst of you."

In so saying, He told us that this healing spirit or principle is actually within man and will work through man. But instead of accepting this, we have tended to surround God with clouds, seraphim and angels, making of Him a majestic, awesome Being whose wrath is to be avoided. We can hardly expect healing from a concept of God such as that. But if we return to the idea of Jesus, that God is an indwelling presence—a renewing principle working in and through man—we begin to see that divine healing is a definite possibility. Sickness and death are not the result of a divine wrath. Rather, they are the result of our failing to understand the true nature of God, and failing to use our divine right to invoke this Spirit through affirmative prayer to bring about healing.

If, as Jesus taught, the spirit or power to heal is available within man, how do we use it? Jesus Himself said that only two important steps are necessary—prayer and faith. He outlined these steps in one astounding thought: "Therefore I tell you, whatever you ask in prayer, believe that you receive it, and you will." He also said: "If you can! All things are possible to him who believes." If a person learns to use properly these two elements of prayer and faith, he can absolutely bring about healing in his life.

You may be wondering about the people who have prayed and had faith and yet were not healed. The answer to this problem ought to be obvious: if a person uses a technique to produce healing, and it doesn't work, he must not be using it correctly. This is the very idea that Jesus had to explain to His early followers. When His apostles failed to heal a lunatic child, He told them, "This kind [dumb spirit] cannot be driven out by anything but prayer." As James said, "You ask and do not receive, because you ask wrongly." We have been of the erroneous opinion that it was necessary for us to come before God with our hat in our hands. Jesus never implied that we ought to be praying beggars. He taught that we are children of God, and should know Him as our Father. And, as children of God, we have the right to decree healing in the way He did. Jesus never begged God to heal a person, because He knew that such begging is not necessary.

Jesus used the right of decree. That is, He pronounced the healing, and it came forth. In doing this, He was using an age-old technique that dates back to Old Testament times. It is found in this passage from the Book of Job: "You will decide [decree] a matter, and it will be established for you." So, when we pray for healing, we must not pray in a beseeching manner. We must affirm the healing life of God, surging through us to do a magnificent healing and cleansing work. If this affirmation is backed with a sufficient quantity and quality of faith, the healing will come forth as surely as the sun rises. The same divine principle that causes the sun to rise will also heal. This principle is God Himself.

Remember that your faith must not be in a God who is distant and apart; nor must it be directed to a God who may or may not heal us, depending on His mood at the moment. Rather, it must be faith that there is a healing principle resident within man and that it will work independently of drugs or surgery. Because this principle is actually God Himself, there is nothing that it cannot heal.

Suppose you feel that your spiritual understanding of God and your faith are just not strong enough to bring about a spiritual healing. Then you wonder if it is wrong to go to a doctor. Many prayers have been answered through the knowledge and skill of a physician. However, there is one cardinal rule to follow: *Go first to God, and then to man as God directs.*

The healing activity of God will work without outside agents. But obviously, all people cannot use it as yet. So the physician sometimes plays an important part in maintaining the well-being of people. Perhaps a time will come when man's understanding of God as an omnipresent help, and his faith in the power of God working through him, will be so great that the maintenance of good health through the application of spiritual techniques will become the rule rather than the exception. And in that day, men will realize what Jesus meant when He said, "He who believes in me

will also do the works that I do; and greater
works than these will he do."

THE MASTER CRAFT OF
Resurrection

A friend called up and asked me when
Easter occurred. I had to ask him to wait a
moment until I checked the calendar. That
seems like a sensible and ordinary thing to do.
Yet, as I began to think about it, it became a
disturbing thing to me to realize that Easter is
an event, as opposed to an experience.

If we regard Easter as only an event, mark-
ing that monumental occasion in history
when Jesus Christ was resurrected from the
tomb of death, we are placing a great limitation upon the entire idea of Easter. But if, on
the other hand, we come to the important,
even profound, realization that Easter is an

eternal experience, then the full significance of the Easter idea comes to us.

When it is properly understood, Easter offers us a blueprint for the master craft of living. An important aspect of learning and practicing the craft of living lies in what we might call the "Easter feeling." Some people have this feeling only on Easter day. Others have it as a part of just knowing that spring has brought green leaves on a lilac bush, the early spring flowers bursting through the soil, and more frequent days of warmth.

All of this is good, and it is all a part of the feeling of Easter. But it is not enough, because it is confined to a certain season of the year. And Easter is not just a date on the calendar. It is not a feeling confined to the springtime. If it is to have real value to us, Easter must be a perpetual experience.

Reverence is an important part of the Easter feeling. It is reverence for the greatest triumph that the world has ever known—a man proving the power of life so greatly that he rises from the prison of a tomb, and becomes the Lord of life. And it is reverence for a living, waking, teeming fragrant earth. It is reverence for the loving, lovable, striving, conquering spirit in man. It is reverence for the potential of life itself—the quality of life that enabled Jesus Christ in His triumphant resurrection to set an example of immortality for all who would follow Him. And therein lies the true value of Easter: the fact that it is an example. Resurrection is not confined to the personal experience of it, as was demonstrated by Jesus Christ. In the day-by-day overcomings and victories that we make in life, we are entitled to use the same power in what we might call our "daily resurrections."

If we wonder by what authority we may assume that we have access to the power of resurrection, let us remember this important biblical passage: "It is the Spirit himself bearing witness with our spirit that we are children of God, and if children, then heirs, heirs of God and fellow heirs with Christ, provided we suffer with him in order that we may also be glorified with him." Jesus was heir to the resurrecting power of life. He used it so magnificently that He was resurrected from the grip of death itself.

That same power is our heritage. We may use it in many areas of victory in our own life. While Jesus Christ's victory over death remains the victory of the ages, there are other resurrections and victories taking place daily in our life. In a real sense, every time we doubt, every time we stumble or fumble or fall but gather our forces to rise and proceed again, we are experiencing something of a resurrection.

One of the prime areas for daily resurrections is in our daily work. There are few jobs where there are no opportunities to improve either the job itself, the way we do it, or ourself in the process of doing it. Resurrection always implies improvement, and many times improvement entails sacrifice and discipline. But sacrifice and discipline were a part of the resurrection of Jesus Christ.

Living could have been easier and longer for Jesus. He could have stayed in Nazareth, run the carpenter shop, married and raised a family, and enjoyed the normal life of a Galilean. But the driving force of His soul would not permit Him to do this. And if any of us sit back in relative contentment and do not answer the call of the driving force of our own soul, then we limit our acceptance of the precious gift of life itself. In the lowliest of tasks there can be found the opportunity to infuse life with the glory of improvement. In that improvement comes a sense of resurrection. One has risen above the lower level of accomplishment to a higher one.

The story was related by Tolstoy, the great Russian writer, of a peasant in Crimea who was forced to stay at the plow on Easter day. Unable to attend church and burn a votive candle there, so important to one of his faith, he fastened a candle to the handle of his plow and kept it lighted while he turned the furrows. Then the work, which had seemed a great hardship, became a sacrament. It was made holy and joyous by the feeling of the presence of God. He plowed the field with a good spirit, and the work was done with care and thoroughness.

While you may not need actually to light a candle at your job, to do it mentally in the spirit of resurrection enables you to make your job a holy task, though it may seem a lowly one. Surely many a cubit is added to our soul when we strive in our daily job to do our work more efficiently, as we strive to discipline the tendency that so many of us have to use only a part of our mind and talent. The tendency of the soul, the driving force within us, is always upward. Even in our most nonplussed, most outraged, most discouraged moments, there is something within us that will reach up and out, and bear us up with it, if we will but permit it to do so.

The Easter feeling that leads into daily resurrections is, of course, a frame of mind, wherein we first relate ourself to our supreme example of resurrection, Jesus Christ, and then relate the example to the various and challenging experiences of our life.

In this respect, I remember a most heart-warming example by Thomas Wolfe in his book "Look Homeward, Angel." Eugene, the hero, and his brother Ben were close. When Ben died, his brother wrote this: "We can believe in the nothingness of life, we can believe in the nothingness of death and the nothingness of life after death, but who can believe in the nothingness of Ben?" Somehow people who have been drawn into some sort of intimate relationship with Jesus Christ, whether it was those in the years when His friends gathered with Him in Galilee or whether in the now—people who have had any kind of experience with the living Spirit of Christ—cannot believe in the nothingness of that relationship.

But such a relationship must not stop here. It must be translated into some definite action of improvement in our life. And if we do this, something happens to us, something in the nature of personal resurrection. We find that the larger life keeps breaking into our little corners. Though we live in one room, the Easter feeling enables us to know that the window of the room opens upon the infinite possibilities of life.

Never minimize the lesser overcoming of life—the daily resurrections. It is doubtful that the great triumph of Jesus Christ could have taken place if there had not been first many lesser overcomings in His life. We all know that there is much to overcome in order to be a master of any sort. Often the artist must employ many techniques in order to achieve the effect he desires. So it was with Jesus Christ. This is how it was that He became the Messiah of men and the Master Craftsman of life.

Some things in the Bible are to be taken literally and some are to be taken interpretively. I choose to take literally the quotation saying that Jesus was "one who in every respect has been tempted as we are." In that case, He must have been tempted to quit a work that had in it so little outer recognition or reward. He must have been irked by the waverings and undependableness of the very human twelve whom He had chosen for His apostles. He must have wished at times to think no further than the radius of His own personal needs and happiness.

Yet it is difficult to associate discouragement or irritation or selfishness with Jesus Christ. Jesus had the ability to be resurrected out of these things as they occurred, and these were His own daily resurrections. It was these daily resurrections that enabled Him to develop the soul power to find revival in Gethsemane and victory at Calvary.

Sometimes life is frightening, and we are inclined to want to run away from it. This is one of the human reactions that many people have. This is what happened at the time of the crucifixion of Jesus. The impact of the crucifixion was shattering. Some of the disciples fled the city. Others gathered together—but behind locked doors, as we are candidly told, because they were afraid that they would be crucified also.

Then came the world-shaking experience: Jesus Christ was no longer dead! They knew He was alive because they talked with Him and heard His words. At times the disciples had difficulty explaining just how the Master appeared to them. Sometimes they felt that they must not touch Him, while at other times He was so earthy that they could offer Him broiled fish. But that He was alive and in their midst, they had no doubt. And this faith transformed them from people who were scared to death into people who were willing to go the length and breadth of the Roman Empire, proclaiming that Jesus was the victor over sin and death.

There was something else that Jesus' followers learned that is of utmost importance to us today. After Jesus was no longer visibly in their midst, they found that they could still have a spiritual rapport, or communication, with the Christ Spirit. They were thus able to maintain a constant relationship with a risen Lord. The ringing message of Easter is that we also may have such a constant relationship.

It is this inner relationship that enables us to have the strength, courage, power, and faith to make daily resurrections. The accumulative power of these daily resurrections, in turn, gives us the ability to rise triumphant over serious challenges, should they confront us in life. To know life in this dimension is to have learned the master craft of living.

If only there were not so many needs for daily resurrections! But it isn't likely that we would appreciate the valid blessings of life if they were handed to us on a velvet pillow. It is good to think of the system of life that has been planned by infinite love and wisdom—that of growing step by step and day by day working for our good as we learn to use it. It is good to watch humanity and to find out by personal experience that we really are bigger than our problems because of the divine dimension of our soul.

When God made you in His own image and likeness, He made a tremendous investment in you. And it is your responsibility to see to it that God gets a good return on His investment. You do this by giving way to the driving force of your soul, as did the Master, and allowing the resurrecting power of Christ within you to enable you to rise in glorious triumph.

First it will be over the little challenges of life, which present themselves daily. And then you will go to the high plateaus of spiritual experience, where your perspective of life is unclouded and complete, where you see life as Jesus Christ saw it—immortal! In the process of this experience, the great transformation occurs in you. You become a risen individual, a more Christlike person. And the great charisma of consciousness becomes the norm of your life.

Let me share with you lines from "Destiny," by Elizabeth D. Schumann:

There is in each of us an inner strength
That gives us power to do what we would
     dare,
A vision that fulfills our every prayer,
A faith that leads us to our goal at length.

All through life's changing hours this truth
     remains;
And though we fail unnumbered times, it
     seems,
We yet may rise and build upon our dreams
The perfect life our destiny ordains.

Printed U.S.A.

123 F-15 M-2-74